Advance Praise

"Through firsthand experiences, Natalia Kaylin details the impact of one's surroundings on their overall quality of life. She takes you through your own home, room by room, detail by detail. The Soulful Home Design Guide *will transform not only your space but the way you live in it."*

—DENISE LINN, author of *Sacred Space*

"If you want to live in an environment that uplifts and nourishes you, this book will show you how. Natalia Kaylin offers a clear framework to transform your home and to support you in living your greatest, most fulfilled life."

—MARCI SHIMOFF, #1 *New York Times* bestselling author, *Happy for No Reason* and *Chicken Soup for the Woman's Soul*

"Whether you are design challenged or an expert in the field, The Soulful Home Design Guide *is an easy-to-use tool to help you mindfully create environments that greatly enhance your life. Who's not into that?"*

—KAREN RAUCH CARTER, author of *Move Your Stuff, Change Your Life*

"In a time of social and economic turbulence, The Soulful Home Design Guide *provides practical advice on creating a sacred space for you and your family. Natalia teaches how your environment can facilitate harmony and stability for you to rest in and to live fully. Thank you, Natalia!"*

—DR. SUE MORTER, bestselling author, international speaker, Founder of Morter Institute for BioEnergetics

"A great guide that will help even the novice create a more inspiring home! Stories of past clients and diagrams throughout the book really help illustrate the power of feng shui and conscious design and bring it down to a practical, thoughtful level. Natalia brings a wonderful soulfulness to this book!"

—MAUREEN K. CALAMIA, author of *Creating Luminous Spaces*

The Soulful Home
Design Guide

Fill Your Home and Life
with Beauty, Love, Peace,
and Prosperity

The
Soulful
Home
Design
Guide

NATALIA KAYLIN

HOUNDSTOOTH
PRESS

The Soulful Home Design Guide
Fill Your Home and Life with Beauty, Love, Peace, and Prosperity

ISBN 978-1-5445-3374-2 Hardcover
       978-1-5445-3373-5 Paperback
       978-1-5445-3375-9 Ebook

For my husband Andy.

Thank you for loving me, encouraging me

and giving me the freedom to fly high.

I love you with all my heart.

Contents

PART III

Putting It All Together

Preface

Picture a Ukrainian village situated on a quaint riverbank—rolling wheat fields and meadows dotted with red poppies, blue cornflowers, and hundreds of other flowers. This is where I was born, and it is the setting for my strongest childhood memory. I was totally entranced by the sweet scent of flowers and the magical cacophony of thousands of insects. Even now when I tune into it, I feel a sense of well-being and joy. This probably explains my love for land, water, and nature, and my wanting to feel a connection and harmony around me.

My family lived in a small brick house. When I was seven years old, my parents bought new furniture and new rugs, and my mom put a few pictures on the walls and placed some decorative ceramic statuettes on the buffet. Twenty-five years later, when I was immigrating to the United States, my mom still had the same furniture and the same decorations placed exactly in the same arrangement. Although many events had happened in her life, the home's décor had hardly changed.

I left my parents' home when I was seventeen, and for the next twenty years I moved from one rental place to another every year or two, never getting the chance to own a home or decorate my own space. My life was minimalistic. I felt that a part of me seriously craved creating a home and being surrounded with beauty and harmony, but I had no idea where to begin and was too afraid to make mistakes and spend money.

Also, I was a technical person, not a creative one—or so I thought. I went through a tough, top technical training at the Physics Department in Kyiv University, and after five years of grinding studies and a boot camp-like environment, I got my MS in electro optics. My specialty was lasers and their various applications. This enabled me to easily get engineering jobs in research and development in the Ukraine and later to work at three startups in the United States. I loved the science aspect of my jobs but despised the cold and impersonal environment of the tech field. After fifteen years working as an engineer, I felt frozen and disenchanted. I knew there was much more to life than what I had experienced.

One day, in the summer of 1999, in a bookstore in Harvard Square in Cambridge, a book literally fell from the shelf right in front of me: *The Western Guide to Feng Shui* by Terah Kathryn Collins. I loved reading that book. It was simple, elegant, and made sense to me. I implemented some recommendations from the book. In a few months I got a raise, and within a year I had met my future husband. At the time, he was divorced and lived alone in a four-bedroom house on four acres of land. He still jokes that he bought the house to entice me. I tell him that he was way more important than the house, but the house was a nice bonus! He had huge plants (raised from seeds) in every room. He also had one bedroom set, two sofas, one kitchen table with four chairs, and nothing else! Twenty years later, we still live in this house and, with time, we have transformed it into a beautiful and soulful space. But something important happened before I met my husband.

Five years before that, in 1994, my life looked very different. I was thirty-two, and I had a special eight-year-old son; unfortunately, I also had an alcoholic husband. Then I had a wake-up call. I was fed up with social and economic instability, and my heart was broken. I could not afford to buy a place to live on my own, and I had no support or hope for our future. I realized if I didn't do something drastic with my life right then, I would never be able to provide a normal life—a good life—for my son and me. As a result, I mustered the courage to leave my husband and immigrate to the United States with my son.

When I arrived in America, I only had a thousand dollars on me. I took a job cleaning rooms in a downtown Boston hotel so my son and I could survive. Fortunately, the economy was good, and five months later I got my first engineering job. Although it was an amazing time of learning and discovery, it was also hard. I didn't have the time or energy to think about the future or what I wanted. Mostly I was just trying to survive.

Four years passed and something happened that made me realize I wanted more than just surviving. It came to me in an unexpected way. One day, as I was driving home from work through the wealthy neighborhood of Weston, I stopped at a traffic light and glanced at the house beside the road. The sun had already set, and the dining room in the house was brightly lit. I could see inside it through the large windows. There was a couple setting the table for dinner, and he came up to her, hugged her, and kissed her in a warm and caring way. It hit me with the force of a thousand bricks. That was what I wanted! The scene and the feeling were exactly how I wanted it to be in my life. Tears ran down my face on my drive home, and my emotions were elevated as I realized that what I just saw was a gift to me from the universe. I realized that for most of my life, my two big underlying feelings were loneliness and unworthiness. In that moment at the stoplight, I felt like love was pouring into me. Feeling this love cracked something in me, and for the first time, I felt good about myself, and I knew, in my heart, that I deserved to have a beautiful, full life and a good man.

This happened six months after I bought my first feng shui book and implemented some of the advice in my apartment. I can't say exactly what caused me to meet my loving, caring husband, but I know it was no coincidence that it all happened within a few months of implementing those changes. Getting clarity on what I wanted, believing that I deserved it, and shifting energy in my apartment toward what I wanted was the *recipe of success* that the universe showed me at that time.

I was inspired and intrigued by the results and felt a strong pull to keep studying feng shui when I moved into my husband's four-bedroom, almost-empty house. I was thirty-seven, and for the first time in my life, I had a beautiful place that desperately needed some furniture and décor. I still had no idea how to do it. When the telecommunication field collapsed in 2002 and the company I worked for ceased to exist, I knew right away that I would not go back to the technical field. Instead, I booked a trip to China to study feng shui with real masters on classical feng shui sites. Studying in China was an experience of a lifetime, and it was extremely useful in helping me separate cultural aspects of feng shui and translate it into the universal language of energy.

I was truly fortunate to study with the best teachers here in the US and around the world. My main teacher and inspiration was Roger Green. In 2003, I took his year-long certification program in New York, which was the most comprehensive in the country at that time. His knowledge was deep, and his passion for feng shui was contagious. In addition to theory, I learned from him on actual sites, houses, apartments, businesses, and medical centers in real-life situations. I opened my practice in 2003 and have been practicing feng shui full-time ever since.

During the first five years, I took a lot of seminars with other beautiful teachers in different parts of the country, learning all the different styles of feng shui. I remember taking a space clearing seminar with Denise Linn. She asked the group a question: "How do you feel when you enter your home?" My answer was "Neutral." I didn't feel a thing! Denise looked me in the eye and said, "This is not about the house, this is about you." The way she said it at that moment, an opening happened, and I saw myself through her eyes. I saw the frozen, overly serious, and unemotional person I was then. Seeing it so clearly made me want to change it. Somehow I knew there was a rich and beautiful world of feelings, colors, shapes, and most of all joy and vitality, out there, and it was so sad not to feel it and experience it fully!

It took me several years of self-exploration, experimentation on my own home, and working with and learning from my clients, but it is obvious now that the process of working on my home and my clients' homes has changed me. My house was an arena and a stage for me to open to my deeper self and my creativity. Slowly, I allowed myself to practice expressing different things through trials and mistakes until I found what felt right. As I was opening and growing as a person, the house was also growing with me, reflecting changes in me and the growth and flourishing of my relationship with my husband. This process of creating a home that supported me and my family at different stages of our lives was part of me becoming more confident, successful, and fulfilled.

Opening to the flow of creativity through working with colors, shapes, textures, and natural objects was very satisfying and gave me a lot of joy. I have realized that I am naturally good at it. I became connected with the magnificence and richness of life. Having learned the secrets and signs, and a language of energy along the way, I take my clients through a similar discovery process to reveal what their joy and fulfillment are and how to bring their surroundings into alignment with them.

My research and engineering background has been immensely useful, because I never take things for granted and can distinguish a real thing from nonsense or superstition. Through working with various aspects of feng shui and as a result of my meditation practice, I have developed a sensitivity and the ability to perceive energy directly. The process is very much alive; there is something new to see and learn every time I work with a property and people. With time, I started to see why and how it works and how energy influences us. Land, buildings, and individual rooms all have distinct energy. Some buildings or even individual rooms feel vibrant and bright, while others can be perceived as sick, stuck, or unhappy. It's an interesting process to find out why they feel this way and what needs to be done to shift the energy and bring balance. Some colors feel joyful and expansive, others sad and constricted, and some are neutral, like there is no life in them. Some shapes feel harmonious while others feel out of sync, as if they take energy from the space. Some textures add softness and smoothness while others add agitation. I hope to be able to pass some of this to you in this book.

I want to take you through a step-by-step process of how to create a soulful home and bring about permanent shifts with lasting results.

Introduction

"I think that when you invite people to your home,
you invite them to yourself."
—OPRAH WINFREY

Your home is an extension of you. It tells your story to the world. Your home can reveal whether you are happy or sad, loved or lonely, content or anxious, confident or shy. If you have a family, it also conveys messages about your family, whether there is harmony and love or distress and pain. We create our environment and make our choices of art, furniture, and accessories depending on our specific state of mind at a particular time. As the seasons of our lives pass, we add more things, and our homes become an accumulation of various emotional states over time, which creates a story. If that story is a happy one, it is fortunate, but it can still get old. Unfortunately, we are often stuck in an unhappy story.

We grow and change, and if our home doesn't reflect those changes, it becomes unsupportive and even draining. And so, we may feel tired, uninspired, or stressed. What if I tell you that you can rewrite and even choose your new story? You don't have to be stuck in an old, sad story, or an old, good story, because it is not your story anymore. If you feel that the time has come for you to dream and live your new story, I am delighted to assist you. We will do it through working on you and with you in your home.

The environment is a dance and interplay of various energies that combine in a harmonious and supportive way, a dissonant and disturbing way, or anywhere in between. Any environment is a result of mixing and combining various shapes, colors, textures, and forms all at once. A piece of furniture or an accessory does not just have energy but, according to quantum physics, is a condensed form of energy. This complex energy, *created by everything in the room,* constantly interacts with our own energy. This *creates an experience and shapes our lives,* whether or not we are aware of it. That is why I emphasize a conscious design with a certain degree of awareness of how things in your environment make you feel. I also emphasize the importance of knowing what you want to accomplish in this phase of your life and, more importantly, how you want to feel. The purpose of this book is to help you *interpret the energies in your home* and *create an environment that interacts with you in a supportive way.*

The ideas described here are backed by science and research: from ancient feng shui to modern environmental psychology. Some concepts I use are researched in clinical trials and rooted in the psychology and biology of how humans constantly adjust to living in fast-paced and rapidly changing modern conditions. The field of epigenetics reveals how the environment is responsible for modifying our genes' expression and therefore our health, strength, and happiness. A home is the biggest part of our immediate environment. I have collected a lot of data based on two decades of working with people and their homes, and I have developed ways to bring these ideas to life in a variety of homes with people of different backgrounds, ages, cultures, races, and incomes. They all wanted the same thing: a home that supports their lifestyle and their goals, and nourishes their soul.

What is a soul? Without going into too much metaphysical or religious explanation, here is my definition of it, or rather the aspect of the soul that is relative to this book. A soul is our inner essence. A soul is experienced through our heart and feelings rather than the mind and mundane thinking, although it does relate to higher modes of thinking, such as insight, inspiration, and creative thinking. A soul is a different dimension of us that is beyond pure logic, reason, and the physicality of the world. The soul relates to our ability to feel love, joy, peace, beauty, compassion, and the overall fullness of life.

We create a soulful home when we design an environment that embraces and reflects this different dimension of us—ensuring a sense of safety, belonging, and nourishment, which is something we all want and need to live a normal life. We are more dependent on our environment than we realize. Not every home will support and nourish us the same way. While we appreciate beautiful things and value special architectural features and décor, we may not feel at home even in the most beautiful or expensive environments if they have no emotional connection to our heart and soul. If there is no such connection, then it is unlikely that we will experience a sense of safety, belonging, and nourishment from the environment.

> *Whether consciously or not, we all want a place where we are able to rest and experience a sense of peace and harmony within. Moreover, we want a place where we can just be ourselves; nothing more and nothing less. This feeling is not loud or big; it is this feeling inside that makes us relaxed, knowing that everything is going to be okay, that we are enough, and we don't need to prove anything to anyone or to ourselves.*

These are the basic things that provide nourishment for the soul. With this knowledge, I want you to approach creating a soulful home.

The soulful home design is an expression that comes from your inner self and demonstrates what your soul truly desires. What you want on a soul level may not be obvious, at first. Trust me, nobody fully knows right away because it is a self-discovery process. Sometimes, this process can be compared to peeling an onion—discovering different layers, moving deeper and deeper toward the core of our inner being. Through a carefully designed structure, guidance process, and clients' stories throughout this book, I hope you will be inspired to discover what you want at this point in your life because knowing that will help you create a home that reflects your desires and manifest them in your life.

When what we want is expressed and satisfied, even partially, we feel at home with ourselves and with the world around us. We feel strong, creative, and content. As a result, we can be more confident and successful in the world. Therefore, creating a soulful home is part of your journey to discover fulfillment in life.

Often it is hard to put into words something that is visually subtle, but there is a sense of *well-being, harmony, and joy* that you feel when your home is designed following the guidance from your soul. I will use the word "joy "many times throughout this book. So we are on the same page, let me describe what I mean. Joy is a soulful emotion. Sometimes it can feel like fullness and blossoming inside and other times like a certain radiance. Often, it is not loud but a quiet feeling of well-being that comes from knowing you are all right and can be yourself. Throughout your home, there is a feeling that things fall into place effortlessly and belong where they are—that the home is alive, and it speaks to your soul. Your guests and visitors feel harmony and a sense of well-being too.

I want to show you how to create something like this. It might seem complicated at first, but if you stay on track and follow the guidance in this book, you will see that it is actually not hard at all. The things that speak to our soul are not complicated. The soul loves simplicity, and so does the soulful home.

This book has two main themes. The first is the elements of a feng shui design and the science of creating balanced and harmonious spaces. The second is uncovering more subtle layers and ingredients of a soulful home. These two themes are not totally independent of each other, as sometimes one permeates the other. Both are necessary to create a holistic environment.

The information presented here will be accessed by both parts of your brain: left and right. Learning how to implement feng shui principles relates to the left part of your brain, which is your analytical and thinking side. Creating an emotion and expressing your inspiration in the space will speak to your right brain, your creative and intuitive side. Both parts are necessary and work together in a perfect and mysterious way to make this work for you.

In Part I of the book, we will set a preparation stage for your journey. In Chapter 1, we will identify energy blockages in your home that correspond to blockages in your life. For some people this might be the most important chapter, as it will allow them to see the main underlying hidden issues like feelings of loneliness, unhappiness, disconnection, or self-judgment. There will be several ways throughout the book to address the hidden issues from different perspectives and move beyond them. Then we will discuss why knowing what you want is a big part of your success. If you know what you want and you set it up right, you can consciously create a home that will support your goals and the vision you have for yourself. You can also aim to energize certain aspects of your life—those that are most important to you at this time—by learning which rooms you should be working on and implementing certain colors, shapes, and elements in your home. We will continue to define a soulful home throughout the book.

Chapter 2 is dedicated to describing feng shui and presenting some of its core principles that we will use throughout the book. Examples of the feng shui Elements in interiors will help to deepen an understanding of the principles. Implementing these time-tested principles will help create a clean and strong foundational structure for the right energy to land in your home. We all know that without a strong foundation, it is impossible to build something that will support us in the long run. Note that the book is geared toward working with feng shui principles and implementing them, rather than teaching a theory.

In Part II, Chapters 3–9 will dive into discussing the seven main building blocks or layers of an environment: decluttering, color, furniture, lighting, art, accessories, and plants. For some of you, decluttering might be a boring subject, or you may think you do not have clutter. But I assure you, it will be useful and necessary to read. It's an important phase of breaking out of stagnation and allowing energy to move, preparing the stage for a new phase of your life. You will learn that furniture, art, and accessories all have different energy. I define and provide several clues about what kind of energy different types of furniture, lighting, art, and accessories have and which ones would best serve to create an environment that is most supportive to your goals. I will emphasize the importance of plants and other natural objects in your home. There is a lot of research published by environmental psychologists and others asserting that people are happier if they are surrounded by plants and natural materials in the home or office.

In Part 3, we will put it all together. Chapters 10–18 are dedicated to guiding you room by room and using feng shui principles and design layers in every room of the home: entrance, kitchen, dining room, family room, bedroom, children's rooms, transitional spaces such as hallways and stairways, and home offices. We will define the meaning of different rooms and engage in creating a home that is healthy, joyful, supports your heart's desires, and furthers your soul's growth.

Some readers might be asking themselves whether the ideas described in this book would be applicable to their home, if a soulful home should be a certain size, or if they can afford to implement ideas from this book. A soulful home concept is scalable and can work with any architectural style, and any size home. It can be created in a mansion or a small studio apartment. I must admit that for different reasons it is more work to create it in a very big or a very tiny home, although I have witnessed in both cases that it definitely can be done.

The budget is also scalable. Although it is good to have a certain amount of money to buy a few pieces of art and accessories, some plants, and even a few new pieces of furniture, the budget should not limit you. Half of the ideas in this book can be implemented without spending money at all if you work with what you already have. Following the exercises and guidance, you will quickly let go of unnecessary clutter while rearranging meaningful items. I guarantee that this will boost your energy and creativity. And if you shop smart, you can certainly create a soulful home without breaking the bank. I will share a few shopping tips along the way. You can do one room at a time or choose to spread this process out for a few years and implement some ideas later when it feels more appropriate money-wise. But if a money issue is one of your blockages (we will discuss blockages in Chapter 1), you definitely want to push yourself a little bit so you get out of the "poverty mindset" sooner rather than later. If you are not worried too much about money and feel that the time is right for you to go full speed, you will likely reach your goals faster. It is certainly your choice. Some of you might be inspired to do a long-awaited remodeling, and I know you will get plenty of support here for your complete home redesign.

Overall, soulful design is not about how much money you spend but how much you can connect with the materials, colors, furniture, and décor items you choose for your home, and whether your décor exudes a positive feeling and a meaningful message for your soul.

This book was written during the Covid-19 pandemic, when many of us spent more time than ever in our homes. Many discovered they loved working from home. It was a surprise for companies to find out that people working from home were as or more productive than they were working in office buildings. People were also happier. Besides the advantages of not commuting and spending extra time with family and exercising, and eating better, I attribute it to the fact that, for most people, their home environment was more supportive than the impersonal and often harsh environment of office spaces. Large tech companies like Twitter and Facebook permanently switched to working-from-home mode, pandemic or not. Many medium and small tech companies follow this model too—at least for now. As time goes by, we may discover some disadvantages of working from home full-time. I worry about the isolation factor and not having face-to-face time with coworkers, especially those coworkers we like.

During the pandemic, many realized the importance of having a supportive environment at home. Many engaged in remodeling and redecorating as a result.

At the end of the book, there is a chapter, "The Home Office," which addresses different scenarios of working from home and creating a supportive work area either in a designated room or in any appropriate part of the room. The rooms where we spend the most time—the bedroom, workspace, kitchen, or whatever room it is for you—are the priority, and this is where I would start.

It is essential to live in an environment that supports your personal energy in the most nourishing way possible. If you have a partner, your living space should support both of you and foster your relationship. If you have children, your home can be a safe cocoon where they grow up nourished and where their choices and creativity are respected and expressed.

> *I know that the impact of a well-designed and soulful home goes way beyond pleasing our sense of beauty and the feeling of harmony. It improves our chances to live a successful, happy, and full life. It boosts our creativity, nourishes our heart and soul, and indirectly strengthens our immune system and improves our health.*

I have witnessed hundreds of people's lives change after they put time and effort into creating a soulful home. Their success stories and their happiness inspired me to write this book.

Here is a simple test. Close your eyes for a moment and imagine coming home. Before you open the door, pause and ask yourself, *How do I feel right now?* Perhaps you feel welcomed, relaxed, and joyful, or do you feel stressed, overwhelmed, and uninspired? Some people feel like there is always too much to do, too many tasks, and too many responsibilities. Some people feel neutral. You don't have to think hard on this one or analyze it. The first feeling that comes through is usually true. I have worked with many people and have seen thousands of stories changed! Like everything in life, it doesn't happen overnight. It's a process, but it can be a joyful, stimulating, and passionate process, during which you will create a beautiful and wholesome home for you and your family and become a more confident, creative, and happier person as a result.

Now close your eyes again, take a few deep, slow breaths, and imagine coming home and opening the door into a beautiful, warm environment where you can just be yourself: free, joyful, creative, and loved. This is what our homes are meant to feel like. This is very achievable. I have done it myself, and many people I have worked with have done it too. Now it is your turn. All the tools and information you need are here, but you are the one who is in charge of putting it to work. I hope you will enjoy this journey with me!

PART I

Getting Started

CHAPTER 1

First Things First

I n this chapter, I am going to share a few fascinating things about your home, your relationship to your home, and how your home can support you on your journey of manifesting what you want in your life, which may include love, success, prosperity, healing, family harmony, and/or personal growth.

These days, many feel that we are here on this planet to evolve, grow, and live fully to our potential. Many are driven to open up to all the incredible facets that life has to offer. When a person grows, their personal vibrational frequency goes up. I often see that if the home doesn't change and still vibrates with the old frequency, our growth becomes stagnant or even stops. It is easy to see when décor doesn't reflect a person anymore. It can be represented in old, tired, and uninspiring paintings, furniture, wall colors, accessories, and definitely clutter. When a person adjusts their environment to correspond to their current vibrational frequency, things start to open up again. More energy flows in their life, and they experience more balance, happiness, healing, and strength.

I am inviting you to take the next step up. I am inviting you to create the environment that represents your *future you*. Yes, it is possible! You can choose your future without limitations, and your home can provide incredible support in your transformational journey.

The ideas described in this chapter took years to realize, observe, and package in a form that is easy to understand and use. Chapter 1 might be the most important chapter for many of you. I hope there will be some "aha" moments and even big realizations.

Creating a Soulful Home Is Much More Than Applying Techniques

When I consult, I assess the property, architecture, and design through my knowledge of feng shui and environmental psychology because I know the tools so well, but I also know that creating an environment is so much more than applying techniques. We must work to respect and honor our home's architectural style, our cultural background, and our taste. But there is more.

As I already mentioned, it is important that we develop a connection with our home. We can begin this with a better understanding of the nature of the rooms and the activities in each room. The rooms have functional and energetic purposes that correspond to various aspects of our lives. For example, it is natural to work with relationships, health, and the inner aspects of ourselves in a bedroom; with family harmony aspects in a family room; and with prosperity and recognition aspects in a dining room. I like to think of the kitchen as the command center and the heart of a home. A bathroom can be transformed into and associated with a relaxing sanctuary. The correspondence between various aspects of our lives and our spaces is natural and essential to us. Yet often we feel lost and don't know where to begin.

Some people follow various design fashions and others try to re-create a look from a magazine. Sometimes it works well because people are intuitively drawn to images that make their soul happy, but it can also lead to a feeling that something is still missing. Often people who don't have time give most of the decision-making privileges to their designers and architects. Don't get me wrong, there are many amazing and talented designers out there, but often I see people regret letting them make all the decisions. They feel they ended up with a home they can't quite connect with.

People who use feng shui from books, especially beginners, often do well and enjoy fresh new perspectives and improvements to their homes' energy. The downside is that beginners tend to implement feng shui principles in a mechanical way, treating the space as various disjoined corners such as a "wealth corner" or a "relationship corner." While this might be helpful, insightful, and fun at the beginning, it may not provide you with a good design or lasting and satisfying results. You must first create a strong foundation and a good energy flow before you start working on improving different aspects of your life. You must see and treat your home as a whole, rather than disjointed areas.

Although certain rules are important and absolutely needed to create a strong foundation, in the end, creating a soulful, holistic, or nourishing home is more than implementing feng shui techniques, environmental psychology concepts, or interior design rules. It is how much you connect with your home and how much your home can reflect to you who you are and what you want to become. This will create a permanent shift in your life. Just as a person thrives when they are cared for, the same happens with the home: your home will care for you, nourish your soul, and project all the love you put into it back to you and more. But first, let us look at how we decorate our homes and identify some of the blockages in our lives that can result.

Identifying Blockages

Our state of mind (positive or negative) and our emotions are reflected in how we decorate our homes. Below is a list of some common blockage scenarios that I often see when working with people in their homes.

I hope you don't feel embarrassed or judged while reading it. You are not alone; everyone has some subconscious issues going on—things that are not quite visible. I treat my clients with the utmost compassion and understanding when it becomes obvious that a certain underlying issue from their life is represented in their home's décor. In fact, it works best to gently but truthfully bring light to these hidden underlying core issues and bring them to the surface. Only then are you able to deal with them. Be assured that I, too, had a few things going on that are listed here. This list is not comprehensive; these are just the most common scenarios. However, it is enough to help you bring awareness to your environment and start recognizing your own blockages that are reflected in your home.

The first set of blockage scenarios relates to how your state of mind influences the environment, which can reveal an underlying issue:

▶ The house has few decorations, despite being occupied for some time. It could be a few years since you moved in, but the walls are still bare and the house furnishing and decorating is still unfinished. This issue usually correlates with indecisiveness—not knowing yourself well enough or not trusting yourself well enough to decorate. In this scenario, you are not open yet to experiencing life fully.

▶ The house is too full. Every possible surface is occupied with keepsakes, decorations, and other small items, and the walls are busy with art and photos. This situation correlates with indecisiveness, too, but also with insecurity and feeling unloved. Decorations and objects provide a sense of comfort and warmth that is otherwise absent from your life. Most likely, as a child you didn't experience enough warmth or affection and felt unloved. There is an emptiness and numbness inside that you are trying to fill.

▶ As a variation of the previous issue, too much clutter could also relate to a number of issues such as avoidance, procrastination, attention deficit, clinginess, inability to let go, and fear of uncertainty.

▶ Art is predominantly dark colored and emotionally sad. Some art depicts autumn scenes of bare trees or dark, stormy water. These choices point to sadness inside, often depression, as well as loneliness and feeling unloved or disconnected.

▶ Pictures of lonely women. Lots of single women are attracted to images of lonely women. Often the women depicted in their art choices are beautiful and strong but rarely joyful. More often they are sad or proud, and this perpetuates loneliness.

▶ Being attracted to black-and-white art reveals that you are a more analytical than emotional person or your ability to feel emotions is blocked.

▶ If your environment doesn't have much color (mostly gray, white, or beige), it means that a certain sweetness and ability to feel joy might be missing from your life. It could also reveal that you follow fashion rather than your heart's passion.

▶ If you have many small art pieces but not a single large one, it shows that you may feel unworthy and never fully go for what you want.

▶ Old, run-down, unmatching, or even broken furniture says that your mind is set on poverty and you are having difficulty letting go.

▶ A perfect, clean, and well-organized house might be great, but not always. Sometimes it points to too much control and an inability to let go, relax, and enjoy yourself. When you become obsessed with cleanliness and organization and every little thing that is "off" bothers you, it reveals that you are out of balance.

▶ If you perfectly match the color of your art with your furniture and walls—rather than highlighting the art—it reveals that you are trying to control too much and not fully open to experiencing all the joys that life can bring.

▶ The same décor for a long time, unchanged, in most cases means that you became stagnant, disengaged, and lost touch with the flow and juices of life.

▶ If the house is uncluttered but the closets are stuffed, it can mean you are hiding behind a façade, you have low self-esteem,

or you have hidden emotional issues but are reluctant to deal
with them yet.

► Children's toys in every room and children's projects and art
on every surface show that you have lost touch with yourself
and children have taken over your universe. Usually an adult
cohabitating relationship suffers in a household like this.

► Piles of mail, magazines, and shoes at the entrance and in the
kitchen point to a lack of organization, which creates an
additional tension and stress in the family.

These last five factors show how architectural, structural, and design
factors may potentially affect you:

► Low ceilings, low light levels, and rooms that are too small
often correlate with low energy, depression, low enthusiasm,
heaviness, and loss of vitality.

► Oversized rooms with high ceilings and white walls correlate
with exhaustion, an inability to relax during the day, and,
eventually, unrestful sleep (for most people, but not
everyone).

► Too many angles in ceilings and walls, sharp décor, or excessively bright paint (especially red colors) may correlate with
agitation, anger, or a feeling of instability.

► Furniture placed diagonally (especially the bed and the desk)
corresponds to a feeling of instability or not being grounded.

► Sitting at your home office or your work area desk with your
back to the open door indicates a sense of nervousness,
feeling unsafe, and not being able to relax.

After reading these twenty examples of potential blockages, you probably have a sense of what you want to let go of in your life. It might be wise to choose two or three aspects to begin with, but if you feel like you want to let go of more than that, go for it! It works differently for different people. Some people, when they see the blockage and how it holds them back, want to change everything quickly, while others are more cautious and prefer to go slowly. Follow your instincts and go for what feels right.

However, it is important not to wait too long before the next step—identifying what you actually want to bring into your life. The way it works is that your new aspiration replaces your old conditioning. Many people get stuck here; they see their problems and blockages, but they go years without addressing them. People pay tons of money to therapists and are still stuck because their environment doesn't change, and the old pattern keeps perpetuating, getting a stronger grip on them.

There is a way out. The next step is to get clarity on what you actually want.

Knowing What You Want by Heart

I often see people living their lives on autopilot. Many have numerous responsibilities, overfilled schedules, unsatisfying relationships, and unfulfilling jobs. One of the reasons people hire me is because feng shui is known for opening the flow of energy for prosperity and success. When I ask my clients what their wealth dreams are or how they would enjoy their money if they had more of it, a lot of people don't know the answer. Many say they want wealth to feel secure, which is true for all of us, but they haven't thought about how they would enjoy their wealth. This is what prevents people from getting significant results. No matter what area of our lives we want to improve, we need to be more aware and more specific with what we want. I have observed so many times that clients who really knew what they wanted got better results, and sooner.

A lot of experts say you need to feel what you want to manifest as though it is already happening. There are times when we can feel it, but it is not sustainable on a continual basis. Manifesting a good life, prosperity, healing, and love is a very old concept, possibly as old as humanity itself. Occasionally, people tap into its power spontaneously, like when I stopped at the traffic light on my drive home and saw—through the window of someone else's home—an expression of the relationship I wanted.

Many experts suggest using positive affirmations and visualizations. As we all know, those work sometimes, but not often because simply repeating even the most beautiful words is not what does it; rather, it is connecting with our dream on a heart level and changing the inner landscape of our feelings. Another big part of it is to release the nagging sense of unworthiness that so many of us have and accept that we are alright and that we deserve to have a good life. It is not so easy, though. Especially when everything in your life screams back at you that you don't have enough, you are not loved, you are having health issues, etc. How can we feel content and happy amidst all that? After years of working on ourselves, some might be able to reach deeper and feel peace and contentment sometimes. It is definitely achievable, but it requires substantial will to manifest real change and growth. It definitely doesn't happen overnight.

What I found to be extremely helpful to forge sustainable change was creating a soulful atmosphere at home and surrounding ourselves with things that transmit the feelings of contentment, happiness, well-being, and prosperity. This way, our inner state of mind and our feelings will be supported on a continual basis.

This works much better than affirmations, because it is tactile for all your senses: you can see it, touch it, sometimes even smell it and hear it, and it is always there for you. As you absorb this positive influence continuously, your home becomes a vehicle for your transformation. This is really the essence of this book.

Let's say you want to work on improving the wealth aspect. However, if your mind and emotional states are set on poverty, I guarantee you will not be able to attract big wealth opportunities. After you do some feng shui and energize your "wealth corner," you might get an unexpected check for a few hundred dollars or even a raise at work which, of course, will feel wonderful, but a huge further development is unlikely if you don't resolve the underlying issue.

To start shifting this, it is useful to understand where the underlying issue is coming from. Typically, it is rooted in a person's family pattern. Your mother or father felt and behaved as though there was never enough money, and you absorbed it. There might be further events in your life that perpetuate and strengthen this belief system. After you recognize it and agree that this poverty mindset might not even be coming from you, but from your parents, you can see that you don't have to stick with it and keep feeding it energetically through your behavior and home décor choices.

Remember my twenty examples of blockages—your home will show you many aspects of your décor that relate to this poverty mindset. After you identify it and follow the next exercise in this book, you can tap into what you really want. If you truly want wealth and are beginning to feel what it means to you, perhaps you can try the following: put an image that resembles wealth in a place where you can see it; buy yourself a new, more comfortable bed that you've wanted for a while; change the ugly, old kitchen countertop that you despise seeing every day; or something similar.

If one of your goals is to have less stress and more joy, you must allow yourself to feel that state of peace, harmony, and joy. It helps to think about times you have had this—while walking on the beach, giving your full attention to a new book, or having a deep conversation with a good friend.

You can also organize your home and infuse it with a sense of peace, beauty, and relaxation. Certain art, colors, shapes, and textures will be instrumental in helping you with this. Otherwise it is all abstract, mental, and distant. You see, it is hard to connect with something abstract, that we don't even feel, so many people just keep going on autopilot and their life keeps going by without them really living it.

When we know what we want in our heart, not just in our head, and when we can be reminded of it by the comfort, beauty, and harmony of our environment, then we are much more open and receptive to it. Sometimes the opening happens very fast, but in many cases it is a process. There are stages of opening to our sense of self-worth and believing in ourselves. I remember many clients' stories and will share a few throughout this book. The two clients' stories below will help demonstrate these concepts in action.

Keira's Story

Keira's story illustrates how fully and completely one can change her story by following her truth. She claims that working on her home through all the different stages of her life was one of the main ingredients in her transformation.

Keira was a stay-at-home mom when I first consulted for her in 2008. She was a delicate and beautiful woman in her mid-thirties. Her husband was making reasonable money, so she was able to stay at home with their eight-year-old son. She was a clothing designer, but she had not worked since their son was born. She hired me because she wasn't happy in her marriage, and she thought I might be able to help fix it. I gave Keira some ideas on how to bring more harmony into her relationship with her husband using certain colors, art, and accessories throughout their home (especially in the bedroom), and she reported that her situation improved.

When I came back a year after our initial meeting, I noticed that she had not fully implemented my advice. While working on the house, Keira felt resistant to altering her master bedroom. She slowly recognized that her relationship was over, but she was afraid to take the big step of ending it. For years, her husband had been convincing her that she was unable to make a living on her own, that it was a scary world out there, and that she needed him to survive. That took a toll on her self-confidence, and her self-worth was low.

After our second meeting, Keira mustered her courage and asked for a divorce. We boosted her career aspect, and despite her fears, she found a job in her field. As I reflect back on our work together, I have to admit, Keira was very dedicated to building her new independent life, and she worked devotedly on implementing changes to her environment and some personal changes as well. She was 100 percent "in," and she didn't want to miss a thing. She always implemented my advice with her own artistic touch and even passion.

Since then, I have seen her once a year for annual updates and fine-tuning of her home's energy to support her growth throughout the year. In those years, I have witnessed remarkable growth. After four years, Keira became a team leader and after three more years, she earned a manager position. She is still delicate and sensitive, but remarkably courageous, straightforward, and fair. She has inspired her younger female employees and acted as a role model for them. Her son has great respect for her, and they have supported and loved each other in this process of becoming financially independent and happy.

The only thing that wasn't working so well was meeting someone she would want to spend the rest of her life with. Keira had been dating over the years and made some nice connections with men, but she felt they were not quite right for her. A couple of years ago, Keira finally moved out of her old house, where she stayed after the divorce, into a new condo in a new town, and it felt like a new beginning. The condo was a perfect fit for her and her son, and we both felt that she would be very happy there.

We discussed that starting from scratch—not bringing any furniture from the old house—was the best way to support this new chapter of her life. She was excited about getting all new art, furniture, and accessories that reflected who she was at this stage of her life, both inside and out. She shared that she knew exactly what she wanted in a relationship, and she felt that the last bits of feeling unworthy fell away as she moved into this new home.

This home was definitely a creation and an extension of her. Not too long after she finished putting her new home together, she met a very kind and supportive man who worked in the financial field and was very well off. She was an avid tennis player and met him at her new town's tennis club. He was also divorced and ready for a new beginning. As I am writing this, I am starting to work with Keira on their newly purchased, incredibly beautiful home. Keira's main goal now is to be fully open to joy in her life. We are painting the rooms in the colors that nourish both of them and give both of them a sense of joy and belonging.

Keira realized that it was a big part of her life journey to discover her worth and her strength through personal and professional growth. As soon as she completed this step and fully realized her worth, she met someone who was right for her. Of course, I had told her how incredible she was all along, but it only works when we believe it and feel it inside ourselves.

There is nothing to lose and life is so much more fun if we let go of feeling unworthy. Having experienced it myself and observed how it works for other people, yes, it requires determination and willpower to stay on track, but it is also embarrassingly simple. You just need to do it! Little by little but consistently doing the opposite of what your old conditioning dictates you do. Redesigning your home and surrounding yourself with things that reflect your sense of self-worth, self-love, vibrancy, and abundance will pay off in a big way.

> *If you truly and passionately want something, the fire of your wanting burns away the old subconscious patterns of unworthiness, loneliness, sadness, stuckness, low energy, chronic sickness, you name it!*

A small success at the beginning must inspire you to keep going, even if your mind tells you "that's enough." And I assure you, it will tell you exactly that.

The negative pattern wants to perpetuate and keep us in it. Some call it self-sabotage. This is exactly why many people stop and some inevitably go back to their old patterns. We have to keep going and building upon our success while being gentle and compassionate with ourselves. We cannot force or control the pace of our transformation, but we can keep opening ourselves to what gives us joy, what makes us feel loved, nourished, confident, and strong. At the same time, we must honor where we are in our journey and never stop believing in ourselves. These are the basic things that, deep inside, all of us desire, but so many don't dare to ask for.

Jennifer's Story

Jennifer's story illustrates how drastically and quickly your life can change if you know what you want and you create a home that supports your dream.

Jennifer owns a company she created and has been running for more than twenty years. She struck me as an energetic and fast-paced person.

She was going through a difficult divorce, had four children aged eight to twenty, and was about to buy a large suburban house for her and her kids. Although she was successful and felt she could accomplish anything, she wasn't happy. She felt something was missing from her life, and she could not quite grasp what it was. She hired me to help with the design of her new house and get some perspective on what was happening in her life.

As we started working together, it was evident that Jennifer's life was out of balance. Everything revolved around work and growing her company. Typically, Jennifer worked twelve- to sixteen-hour days, every minute scheduled with meetings and commitments. She confessed that she often worked through the night to meet a deadline. Although she was a great mom and participated in her children's numerous activities, everyone in her family seemed stressed and overscheduled. She was running her home just like her business: everything was fast, efficient, and super structured.

Though she enjoyed being a successful entrepreneur, it was clear to me that she had lost the ability to relax and experience the other joys in life. After I shared some of my observations with her, she decided that it was time to attend to her heart's needs and find her joy again. I was amazed at the amount of commitment and focus she gave to this task. Despite her busy schedule, she met with me three to four hours every couple of months for a year and a half.

In the new house, Jennifer was able to fully unleash her creativity. It is rare that I see anyone so passionately enjoy working on their home the way Jennifer did. She and her ex-husband had very different styles and ideas on how they wanted their home to look. Before, she had delegated the job to designers and gave into her husband's demands on interior design and colors. For the first time in her life, she felt free to express her artistic side and put her heart and soul into creating her new home. She allowed me to guide her, as she was discovering what made her feel joyful, relaxed, fulfilled, and loved. She said that she cried when she saw the way her bedroom color came out after it was painted. We picked the color that resonated the most with what was happening in her heart. It was pink.

Every time I saw her, she was feeling happier and lighter, and it was reflected in her relationships with her children. They were changing as well. They became more creative, relaxed, and happier too. They hung out together as a family more than ever, because the space was harmonious and conducive to family gatherings. Soon after we started working together, she met someone special and fell in love; her new relationship supported her new version of herself. She looked twenty years younger and was experiencing all the facets of being in love and being loved.

Jennifer still works a great deal, but she discovered that there is so much more to life than a career and professional success. Through working on her home, she discovered the previously hidden gems of her soul and was able to quickly rewrite her story by prioritizing her home and putting her will and passion into the process. Her passion is contagious. She keeps inspiring her children and everyone around her to live fully and be in charge of their lives.

Identifying What You Want

I highly recommend that you write down three to six new things that you want to bring into your life. Choose a time when you are not pressed with responsibilities, perhaps on the weekend. It may help to go for a walk or do something that brings you joy and relaxation before you tune into your desires.

This exercise works best if you write your list, rather than just thinking about it. If you are interrupted by thoughts about why you can't do something, have something, or experience something you want, just let them go and keep writing. Here are some examples, but what you write should be personal to you. Your list might look like this:

- ▶ I want to bring more harmony and intimacy into my marriage.
- ▶ I want to experience more joy in my life.
- ▶ I want to feel financially secure and stop worrying about spending money.
- ▶ I want my children to be more independent and responsible.

Or like this:

- ▶ I would like to improve my health and energy. I want to feel vibrant.
- ▶ I would like a career change. I want to discover my passion and be able to make money while doing what I love.
- ▶ I would like to have more like-minded friends.
- ▶ I would like to have more time for myself, including spending more time in nature.
- ▶ I would like to travel to exotic countries like Thailand or Bali.

Or like this:

- ▶ I would like to meet my soulmate.
- ▶ I would like to live with him or her in a beautiful new home.

▶ I would like to lose thirty pounds and feel vibrant and comfortable in my body.

After you write these, spend a few minutes or longer, if you wish, on each one of these aspects. Allow yourself to experience and embrace how it would feel if you already had what you want. Feelings such as warmth, clarity, joy, strength, and confidence may come up. You may feel elevated. You can even rewrite your statements, if you wish, using better and more precise words. The words should feel right and resonate with your heart. I suggest, at this time, that you choose no more than three most important things to concentrate on while working on your home and following the information in this book.

Now it is time to exercise the left part of your brain and learn a few basic feng shui principles. This will be useful for you further along in the book when we work on individual rooms. The knowledge of these principles will help you understand how to work with different types of energy in your environment and how these energies may influence you.

CHAPTER 2

Feng Shui Principles

About Feng Shui

The practice of feng shui originated in China and can be traced to 4,000 BC—perhaps even earlier. Most of the techniques practiced by feng shui masters today were recorded in the last 1,500 years. In modern times, as in ancient times, the practice is aimed at harmonizing people with their environment by understanding the forces of nature and aligning themselves with these forces. In China, the location of the dwellings, tombs, and entire villages and cities were determined by the presence of landscape features such as mountains and hills, ocean and rivers. We are deeply interconnected with our environment, and our survival and thriving depend on it. If you think about it, even in the Stone Age some form of this practice must have been used, since the survival of a Stone Age person would depend on the type and location of the cave they chose.

> *In essence, feng shui is the science and art of creating beautiful and balanced environments that are in harmony with people and nature.*

Feng means "wind" and *shui* means "water"—two forces of nature that signify the flow of energy in the environment and interconnectedness of all things visible and invisible.

On a practical level, today feng shui is used to balance all the influencing factors in the environment to create the most optimal space for the occupants. It is still used for auspicious site selection and determining the best placement of a house on a plot of land. However, because most people don't have much choice in finding the land and freely positioning the house on it, in most cases, the discipline addresses the interior and exterior design of the home. The design is aimed not only at how the environment looks, but how it feels and how it influences us on a subconscious level.

Feng shui is a complex body of knowledge developed by different masters over a long period of time. There are many schools and techniques that have been tested by age, but in this book I'll be addressing only basic (fundamental) feng shui techniques and environmental psychology concepts that will help with our goal of creating a soulful home.

We have already started the discussion that creating a soulful home is much more than applying techniques mechanically because techniques must be combined with emotion and intuition—not only to provide a sustainable foundation but to create a connection to a home.

Form school feng shui examines the landscape features such as mountains, hills, oceans, rivers, streets, surrounding buildings, and the energy flow throughout it. It also assesses characteristics of the plot, the architectural design of the house, room placement, furniture placement, and overall design features. All is taken into account to understand and optimize the flow of energy in the environment. It is the most practical and widely practiced system we will use and engage with in our process.

Yin/yang analysis is used to determine if an environment's energy is out of balance and is aimed at achieving balance.

The Five Elements system addresses five different types of energy or universal forces that are parts of the whole. Knowing the nature of the room and what type of activity is done there will provide an understanding of what type of energy is needed in a certain space. Introducing the right type of energy can balance and enhance our experience in each area and neutralize negative influences.

The Bagua or Eight Life Aspirations system deals with different energies that are represented by different compass directions and their relation to various aspects of our life. All eight compass directions have different subtle properties, which the Bagua relates to specific personal factors such as career, self-development, family harmony, health, prosperity, recognition, personal relationships, children, and helpful people (mentors, clients, and ancestors). Depending on what aspects need to be enhanced, a corresponding compass sector of a home or business can be targeted and energized.

At some point, you may want to explore other techniques such as Flying Star, Ming Gua, and Bazi (see my website www.nataliakaylin.com for descriptions of these techniques), but they are outside our scope right now.

A Special Note on Chi Energy

Whenever I refer to "energy" in this book, I am actually referring to "chi," which is translated from Chinese as a life force. In Indian tradition this energy is called prana. It is a very mysterious, partially cosmic, partially earthy energy that everyone can feel and experience every waking moment, yet it is difficult to grasp what it is with our mind alone. If this energy flows unobstructed inside and around our body, we feel healthy, vibrant, and peaceful. If its flow is obstructed in any way, we feel out of balance physically and emotionally, and if left unattended, eventually the result is pain and disease. Acupuncture directly addresses and restores the chi flow in the human body and so does rest, exercise, proper diet, and satisfying our emotional needs.

A similar thing happens in the environment.

If the optimal chi energy flow in our home or any of the rooms is obstructed, we feel stagnant, unhappy, tired, and uninspired. When the flow and the quality of the energy is restored, we feel stronger, happier, more creative, and productive.

Simply put, we can refer to this chi energy as a measure of the vitality of the space. In a way, working with a home feels like performing acupuncture on the building or an individual room. We do it by removing blockages, redirecting and enhancing the flow and quality of energy, and proper placement of the furniture and décor.

About Environmental Psychology

Environmental psychology is a multifaceted discipline that has been developing since the 1950s. It is based on research and studies of how people interact with their environment and how the environment affects human behavior and welfare.

The field defines the term *environment* broadly and includes natural environments, social settings, built environments, and learning and informational environments. The scope of environmental psychology goes far beyond the interaction between people and buildings. That being said, part of the research is aimed at studying the behavior of the occupants of buildings including homes, offices, institutions, hospitals, hotels, etc., and learning what enhances the occupants' physical and mental health, as well as what improves creativity and productivity.

> *Studies and trials have found that a greater connection to nature is important to human beings. Using natural materials, plants, natural (or close to natural) lighting, and certain colors in homes, offices, and institutions brings a greater sense of well-being, productivity, and overall happiness.*

There is also a specific branch of environmental design that addresses sustainability and aims to reduce negative impacts on the greater environment by reducing consumption of nonrenewable resources, minimizing waste, and improving a building's performance. There is a lot of emphasis lately on using healthy materials in buildings, furniture, and décor items versus materials that outgas or use components detrimental to human health.

Some of the décor and color recommendations in this book are rooted in various aspects of these studies. The parallels and similarities between certain facets of feng shui and environmental psychology are striking at times. In a way, both disciplines (ancient and modern) validate and enrich each other.

Now I want to introduce you to or remind you of these three basic and essential feng shui principles. They are integral for our purpose of creating a wholesome, beautiful, and happy home.

Yin/Yang Principle

Yin and yang are opposing energies, although we can experience them only in comparison with each other. Some examples are: feminine and masculine, low and high, soft and hard, dark and bright, wavy and angular, ornate and plain, still and active, dim and bright.

If a house or a particular room has low ceilings, not enough natural light, walls painted neutral colors, and the décor is predominantly dark, this would be an extreme yin. After some time living in such an environment, we would feel low, uninspired, and even depressed. If you add clutter on top of it, the results could be quite disastrous.

If a house has very high ceilings, marble floors, skylights, too large or too many windows, angular architectural features, white walls, and light-colored furniture, this would be an extreme yang. Although it may seem attractive at first, it would be hard to get rest in a house like this and, with time, we would become overwhelmed, agitated, and ungrounded.

People feel the most comfortable in their space when these opposites are close to being balanced. Depending on the nature of the activities for which the room is used, we would want the energy to be either balanced or slightly more yin or more yang. In a family room, for example, we would want to achieve a good balance of yin and yang since it is the room where we want family members to relate to each other in the most harmonious way. In other rooms, like the dining room, where we expect to be consuming food and socializing, a more active and therefore more yang energy is appropriate. In the bedroom, we would benefit from restful energy, and therefore the balance should shift toward yin.

Diagram 1: Yin/yang symbol

This symbol emphasizes the constant flow and transformation of yin and yang. Like day transforms into night, summer into winter, joy into sadness, excitement into relaxation, our life will flow and change from more active to more restful phases several times during our lifetime and even during the day. You are going to feel supported and aligned with your goals if your environment reflects changes in your life. A simple example is when we rearrange our closet from winter to summer clothing and back or use seasonal plants and flowers throughout the year.

It is also a good idea to make adjustments to your décor depending on where you are in your life journey. For example, if you want to do something that requires an action like start a new business, exercise more, or generally get you out of stagnation, it would be a good time to introduce more yang (energizing) colors and décor elements in your home. On the other hand, if you feel burned out, agitated, or stressed, you would benefit from more yin (soothing) colors and décor elements in your home.

In a few years, when this phase passes, you adjust again. It is nice when your home supports you in this way that is not static but instead reflects the changes you are going through. In Part III, we will discuss in detail using yin and yang elements in each room of your home. Yin and yang aspects are not absolute; rather, they are always relevant to each other and compared to each other. There are extreme expressions of these aspects and everything in between. The more detailed expression of energy is the Five Elements system.

The Five Elements System

The Five Elements represent five different types of energy.

Wood is rising energy, Fire is expanding energy, Earth is sinking energy, Metal is gathering energy, and Water is floating energy.

In terms of the practical application of the Five Elements:

Wood is used in places where we need to uplift the energy. Wood represents growth and movement and is associated with prosperity and wealth. Examples of the Wood Element in interiors are plants, vertical shelves, columns, or any tall vertical objects, new furniture made of real wood, pictures of trees and plants, wallpaper that depicts vertical features or plants, and the color green.

Fire is used to bring expressions of beauty, joy, excitement, and enthusiasm. Fire is associated with happiness, fame, and reputation. Examples of the Fire Element in interiors are the stove; a fireplace; lighting; candles; triangular shapes; and red, maroon, hot pink, and orange colors.

Earth is used to bring a sense of stability, nourishment, and support. Earth is associated with relationships and the mother of the family.

Examples of the Earth Element in interiors are granite countertops; tile; ceramic dishes; porcelain vases; clay pots; sofas; chairs; square shapes; and yellow, tan, and brown colors.

Metal is used for expressing refinement and creating a concentration of energy. Metal is associated with creativity, helpful people, and the father of the family. Examples of the Metal Element in interiors are clocks; metal wall décor; fireplace tools; round shapes; and white, gray, and metallic colors.

Water is used for bringing the energy of relaxation and adventure. Water is associated with career and wealth. Examples of the Water Element in interiors are pictures with water in them, aquariums, water fountains, organic wavy shapes, and blue and black colors.

The Five Elements relate to each other in a supportive (also called "creative"), diminishing, and destructive cycle.

A **supportive (or creative) cycle** involves elements that support or create each other. Wood needs water to grow; Fire is fueled by Wood; ashes are transformed into Earth; by condensing, Earth produces Metal; Metal is dense enough to hold Water.

For example, if we need more of the Wood Element in a room, we could add Water to make Wood stronger. And if we need to strengthen Metal, we could add the Earth Element.

A **diminishing cycle** contains Elements that deplete each other. Fire consumes Wood; Earth reduces Fire; Metal empties Earth; Water takes away from Metal; Wood drains Water.

A **destructive cycle** happens when Water puts Fire out; Fire melts Metal; Metal cuts Wood; Wood saps nutrients from Earth; Earth consumes Water.

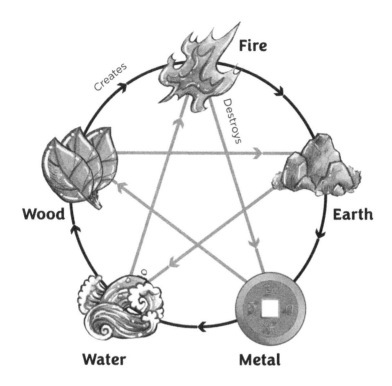

Diagram 2: Five Elements interaction cycles

Both diminishing and destructive cycles are used to reduce Elements. The diminishing cycle is a more harmonious way to reduce an Element than the destructive cycle, but both ways can be used to minimize the Elements that are in excess.

For example, if we have too much Wood, we can add Fire, which will weaken Wood in a harmonious way. Alternatively, we can add Metal to cut Wood or Earth to exhaust it. Let's say there is a room in the house with wood panels, wood ceiling, and wood shelves. It would feel overwhelming, and to balance the room we could use the color red in a piece of art or a rug. We could also use accessories made of metal and earth, whichever Element would be the most appropriate.

If the Metal is too strong, adding Water will weaken it, adding Fire will destroy it, and adding Wood will exhaust it. In an actual room, if all the walls are white and the furniture is gray, that would mean too much Metal Element. While it might look contemporary and functional, it would feel cold, uninviting, and unemotional. To reduce the Metal Element, we would introduce art or accessories that contain Fire, Wood, or Water Elements, whichever is the most appropriate for the space according to the nature of the room, the Bagua, and your aesthetic sense.

Another example of imbalance in the environment that I see quite often is when there is too much Earth Element. This would look like a beige-painted room with brown sofa and chairs, and a tan rug. You can add a stone fireplace to it just to complete the picture. The way to reduce Earth would be to bring in green, gray, or blue—perhaps even repainting the room—as well as adding plants, images of water, and things made of metal.

Sound too complicated? Fear not. As we move from room to room, there will be more examples and it will become easy. The important thing to recognize is if the Elements are out of balance with too much or too little, we will feel out of balance as well. The Five Elements system offers a harmonious way to bring the environment back into balance.

Below, I've listed some of the effects of elemental energy imbalances that we may experience in our environments.

Wood

If it is in balance, Wood represents growth, spontaneity, expansion and innovation.

If there is not enough Wood Element, we may experience a stagnation of growth, heaviness, or a loss of spontaneity.

If there is too much Wood, it may result in feeling hyperactive, overly committed, and overwhelmed.

Fire

If it is in balance, Fire represents action, passion, and leadership.

If there is not enough Fire Element, we may feel a lack of energy or joy and emotional coldness.

If there is too much Fire, we may experience impatience, aggressiveness, or compulsiveness.

Earth

If it is in balance, Earth represents stability, reliability, practicality, nourishment, and sensuality.

Too little Earth Element may elicit instability, irritability, worry, and a lack of trust.

Too much Earth would strengthen the feeling of being overly conservative, heavy, and stagnant.

Metal

If in balance, Metal represents clarity, good organization, no clutter, and refinement.

If the Metal Element is on the low side, we may experience confusion, indecisiveness, and a lack of structure.

Too much Metal would make us feel rigid, cold, unemotional, and overly controlling.

Water

If in balance, Water represents relaxation and flexibility. It supports the intuitive and artistic aspects of our personality.

If the environment doesn't have enough Water, we may feel stressed, anxious, and dry.

Too much Water Element may translate into fearfulness, depression, and an inability to act.

As we go through different rooms in Part III, I will discuss what type of energy we want to create in each room and the colors, furniture, art, plants, and accessories in the form of the Five Elements that produce the right balance for each space.

The Bagua or Eight Life Aspirations

The *Bagua* literally translates from Chinese as "eight symbols." Those eight symbols are trigrams that consist of various combinations of solid (yang) and broken (yin) lines. They represent different forces of nature and some fundamental principles of reality that are well described in *I Ching*. There are correspondences to the trigrams in nature, seasons, planets, human body parts, family members, time of day, and more. In feng shui, we use some of these aspects, such as compass directions, nature, seasons, time of day, family members, health, and personality type.

As we go through the design of the rooms, we will consider some of the relevant applications of the Bagua.

The Bagua's central aspect that is derived from the meaning of the trigrams is eight compass directions. A clever feng shui design would depend on the direction the room is in. Remember the definition of feng shui has to do with living in harmony with nature. Clearly, we have different experiences in a southern room, which is filled with sun most of the day, and a northern room, where the sun never shines. This is if we live in the Northern Hemisphere, of course. In the Southern Hemisphere, the experience is the opposite and the Bagua should be adjusted accordingly. In this book, we are discussing the Northern Hemisphere Bagua.

For example, if our kitchen is in the northeast, east, or southeast, we will be energized in the morning by the wakeful energy of the rising sun as we have our cup of coffee and breakfast before going to work. If, instead, our kitchen's windows are in the west or northwest, we will experience the gentle, warm, and relaxing influence of the evening sun while cooking and eating dinner.

It doesn't seem like a big deal, but these different experiences influence our energy little by little every day. Over time, there will be a cumulative effect. If the room's location and design support our energy in a certain way, it will correlate with strengthening certain aspects of our lives.

The correspondences between compass directions and life aspects such as relationships, prosperity, and family harmony suggest working in those areas of our home to remove stagnation and infuse it with new healthy and vibrant energy.

The elements of design such as colors, furniture, art, accessories, plants, and some special objects are used to create this new and supportive energy.

The Meaning of the Trigrams and Directions

Some of the aspects of the trigrams are more useful and applicable for interiors than others. The most applicable are the Five Elements, which we will translate into the elements of design and colors. Knowing the correspondence between family members and each direction can be very useful too. If a family member is having a problem of some kind, they would benefit from additional energetic support. It is good to know which direction is associated with father, mother, daughters, and sons. Diagram 3 depicts the classical feng shui Bagua.

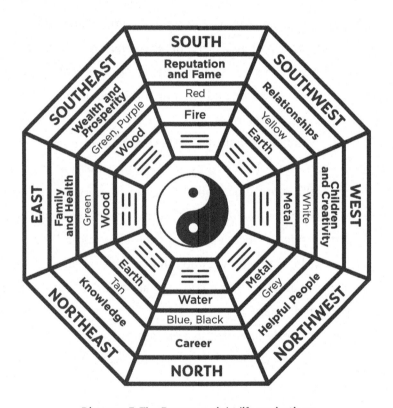

Diagram 3: The Bagua or eight life aspirations

East is an aspect of the **Thunder trigram**, also known as "**the Arousing.**" This trigram has one solid yang line at the bottom and two broken yin lines on top of it. The image is of a rapidly rising energy, powerful like thunder in the spring. East represents **growth, family, and health**. Other aspects of the Thunder trigram are spring and early morning. The member of the family is the oldest son. Wood Element represents this rising energy and according to the Five Elements supportive cycle, Wood needs Water to grow. This is why Elements of the east are Wood and Water, and the colors are blue and green. More detailed information on Bagua corresponding colors and their use will be presented in Chapter 4.

Southeast is an aspect of the **Wind** trigram, and it is called "**the Gentle**." This trigram has one broken yin line at the bottom, and the image is of a gently rising energy penetrating through two solid yang lines. The sun is still on the rise when in the southeast, therefore energy is rising too. We want our wealth to grow steadily, which is why this trigram is associated with **prosperity and wealth**. Other aspects of the Wind trigram are late spring, early summer, and late morning. The family member is the oldest daughter. The Element of the Wind trigram is gentle Wood. Wood doesn't grow without Water. Both Water and Wood are native Elements of the southeast, and the corresponding colors are blue and green.

South is the aspect of the **Fire** trigram, and it is called "**the Cling-ing**." This trigram consists of two solid lines on the outside and a broken line inside. It represents **fame** and **reputation**. It also relates to beauty, brightness, and joy. The energy is expansive and high, but the yin line in the middle points to a vulnerability inside. The peak is unstable, and so is our fame. It is the energy of midsummer and midday. The family member is a middle daughter. The Element of the Fire trigram is Fire. The color is red or orange. Wood feeds the Fire, so a second color of the south is green.

Southwest is an aspect of the **Earth** trigram. It has three broken yin lines and is called "**the Receptive.**" It is the pure form of yin energy. It represents feminine strength, receptivity, nurturing, and devotion. This is why southwest is associated with **relationships** and **the mother**. It is the warm and nourishing energy of the afternoon and late summer. The Element of the southwest is Earth. The colors of Earth Element are yellow, tan, or terra-cotta. Fire creates Earth, therefore Fire Element and the colors red, orange, or pink support the energy of the southwest as well.

West is an aspect of the Lake trigram, and it is called "**the Joyous.**" It has one broken line on top of two solid lines and has connotations of joy, pleasure, and all good things in life. It is in the evening, when the sun is in the west, that we enjoy spending time with family, eating food together and playing with our children. This is why the west relates to **children** and **creativity**. Additionally, the youngest daughter, the joy of the family, is represented by this trigram. The Element of the west is Metal. The colors are white, gray, silver, and gold. Metal is created by Earth, therefore the earthy colors yellow, tan, and terra-cotta are appropriate here too.

Northwest is an aspect of the **Heaven** trigram and is called "**the Creative.**" It consists of three solid lines and is pure yang energy. It represents **helpful people** and the **father**, the breadwinner, or the **head of the family** (this can be a woman, of course). The Element of the northwest is Metal. All the Metal and Earth colors are appropriate in this area, but the energy of the northwest is very different from the playful and joyful west. It is a more serious area that relates to your spirituality, ancestors, mentors, or everyone from whom you receive blessings and guidance.

North is an aspect of the **Water** trigram. The solid yang line inside of two broken yin lines on the outside represents strength and flexibility. It is called "**the Depth.**" As a meandering river, it represents our **path in life**, **our potential**, and the **career** aspect. The season associated with this trigram is winter, and the time of day is night. The family member is the middle son. The Element of the north is Water. Water is supported by Metal, therefore colors that resonate with north are black, blue, white, gray, and silver.

Northeast is an aspect of the **Mountain** trigram. The solid line on top of two broken lines is interpreted as the sky above the accumulated earth, portraying the image of the mountain. It is called "**the Stable or Still**" and represents **knowledge, self-development**, and **meditation**. The season of the northeast is late winter and early spring; the time of day is late night and early morning. The family member is the youngest son. The Element of the northeast is Earth, and corresponding colors are yellow or tan. The nature of the northeast is such that besides all the earth colors, greens and blues are appropriate here too.

Center of the home represents the health and well-being of the household. It is presented on the Bagua Diagram by the yin/yang symbol, which describes wholeness and totality of energy.

We will discuss the application of the yin/yang, Five Elements, Bagua, and colors in Part III when we work with each room. For now, I want you to see the example of applying the Bagua to the floor plan.

Applying the Bagua to a Floor Plan

The best time to apply the Bagua and other principles is when we build a house or do a big remodeling. Then we can create a floor plan with a certain flow to the rooms that will harness the natural energy in the most beneficial way. And if we don't have the luxury of building our own house, the next best solution is to improve the energy of each room. You will find a lot of ideas on "how to" in the following chapters.

To apply the Bagua to a floor plan, you need to do a compass measurement.

When you align the red needle with the north, the line that is perpendicular to the front of the building is your building facing direction. For the house in Diagram 4, it is the line that is perpendicular to the front and back walls of the house and crosses the center of the floor plan. In this floor plan, the line crosses the west direction of the compass; therefore, the facing direction of the house is west. The next step is to draw the eight directions from the center. It is like superimposing a compass on the floor plan. You can also use the app or Google Maps to determine your home's facing direction and create a Bagua on the floor plan. It will look like the diagram below.

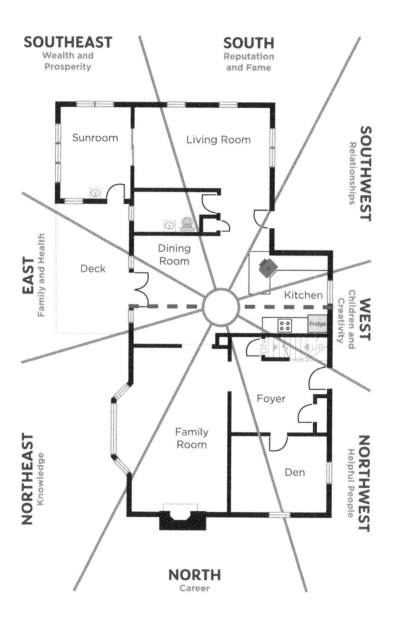

SOUTHEAST
Wealth and
Prosperity

SOUTH
Reputation
and Fame

SOUTHWEST
Relationships

Sunroom

Living Room

EAST
Family and Health

Deck

Dining
Room

Kitchen

WEST
Children and
Creativity

Fridge

UP

DN

Foyer

NORTHEAST
Knowledge

Family
Room

Den

NORTHWEST
Helpful People

NORTH
Career

Diagram 4: The Bagua applied to a floor plan

Sometimes practitioners use nine squares instead of eight radial segments and it is totally fine. I adopted a radial map that resembles a compass. It feels more natural because energy doesn't travel in squares, but rather, comes from all eight directions toward the center of the house. Note that the center is not a dot; it is a circle or oval that is about one ninth of the total area of the floor plan.

Now, let's dive into the seven main building blocks of creating a soulful home.

PART II

The Seven Building Blocks of Creating a Soulful Home

CHAPTER 3

Building Block One— Decluttering

For some people, decluttering is a huge issue, and for others, it is natural and not a big deal. Some might even find the subject boring and unappealing. This chapter, however, is a must-read because it is not just typical clutter I want to address. Some of it is not what you may expect, and it is an important part of our process of creating a soulful home.

The truth is we have big houses and a lot of things in them. Many of us have full basements, some have full garages, and a lot of us have filled every single closet.

Skipping decluttering is not an option. Period. You cannot substitute this step with something else. You need a strong, healthy foundation for your home and your life. If you avoid it, whatever you do in your home will be like building a castle on sand.

Whatever you create will not last long, and with time, your problems will only get worse. You will develop all kinds of avoidance mechanisms, and your life will be less fulfilling. There will be other implications as well, but you get the idea. If you are truly ready for change and want new things to come into your life, you have to let go of the past and what does not suit you anymore.

Here is a good general rule to work with. Look at and feel the item, whether it is a piece of furniture, an accessory, cookware, a book, or clothing—it doesn't matter what it is, just feel it. How does it make you feel? Do you feel expanded or contracted? Do you feel joyful or sad? Do you feel confident or anxious? Do you feel stressed or relaxed? Do you feel wealthy or poor? Does it feel like the old you or the new you? It could be quite subtle and hard to put into words, but if you don't like the way it makes you feel, then don't keep it!

Start with the kitchen. The kitchen is the heart of the home, and we spend a good amount of time in it. The main clutter spots are the fridge and the pantry. Get rid of all the old, expired food and physically clean the fridge. The same with the pantry. It makes us stressed if it contains too much stuff, and we keep stuffing it in because we don't even know what is in there anymore. You will feel awesome if there is space in the fridge and pantry and you can see everything and find things easily. Having too many items in the fridge or pantry can increase your stress by making finding things difficult and, for some, relates to being overweight. And if you are ambitious, you can go through all the cabinets and do the same. If you go through your cabinets, you will find several things that you don't use any longer like cups, cookware, and attachments to various appliances. Some of the appliances might be gone by now. You may not even remember exactly what you have stored on those higher shelves that are out of reach. I call this process "presencing," which means that I am aware of what items are present in my space. Knowing what you have and where you have it helps you feel grounded and relaxed. Your energy will open and spread because you will feel that you are in charge! It's literally like the saying "getting monsters out of the closets." In this case, too much "unpresenced" stuff is the monster that is weighing you down.

The bedroom is another important area for decluttering and presencing. The bedroom relates to our inner sensitive self and our relationship. Our energy is open and vulnerable when we are asleep. Having too many things on our nightstands or shelves, including medicines and books, prevents us from fully letting go and having a restful sleep. Besides, things collect dust, which may trigger our immune system response and, therefore, allergies and inflammation. The fewer things we have in the bedroom, the better our ability to get deeper sleep and better rest. When our bedroom is filled with beautiful energy that can move freely, we feel safe and nourished.

Clothing is such an important aspect of our lives. We regularly wear certain clothes, while we wear others only once or twice, and they just keep collecting dust and taking up space in the closet. Perhaps they even trigger a feeling of guilt. The reason is simple: some clothes not only reflect who we are but make us feel loved, empowered, strong, and vibrant. It could be a combination of their color, shape, and fit, but wearing them always generates a good feeling. They support our energy. It should be easier to let go of clothes that don't make us feel this way, right? It is unlikely that the feeling is going to change with time! Freeing the space will make you more ready for something new in your life.

The entrance is where energy transfers from outside and distributes throughout the house. The entrance should welcome your guests and greet you with a sense of peace and warmth. Do you know how many people tell me that the moment they enter their house they feel stressed? It feels as if there is always too much to do and there is no time and space to rest! If this is how you feel upon entering your home, I bet you will find an accumulation of clutter in various places. I see how it crushes people.

> *The underlying message that clutter sends is that you have to do something. This is a source of continuous stress.*

So clearing the entrance and entrance closet is a huge positive step, but do not stop there.

A home office definitely needs a lot of attention. If you work from home, then prioritize it. The accumulation of stuff blocks your productivity, creativity, health, and prosperity!

Often, people get half done, start feeling good, and stop. Trust me, if you complete the task, then the positive feeling is much stronger. It is transformative! Address the areas you don't see too often, such as spare bedrooms, basements, garages, and attics. The truth is, if you haven't been using those things for a decade or more, you don't need them! But storing excess things makes you feel guilty, heavy, depressed, and stressed.

I am not a clutter consultant, but I know the effects of it very well. Besides a general malaise that clutter creates, I see a correlation between clutter in the bedroom and health or relationship. Clutter in the family room influences family harmony, and clutter in the dining room affects social status, just to name a few effects. I hear it is quite motivating for clients to declutter when I mention these correlations.

We all want to feel vital, joyful, and creative. The first rule of vitality is less stuff and more free space. A sufficient amount of free space supports energy flow through the space.

For some people, decluttering is a lifesaving and transformative process. You can keep thinking about it, taking courses, and buying books on decluttering, but at some point, you need to get into your warrior mode and attack it. Be ruthless; you are fighting for your health and well-being.

Keeping our home physically clean is a big contributor to creating a healthy environment. When dusting, clearing off the shelves, reaching all the corners, and getting behind and underneath the furniture makes a big difference. Once in a while I like to use a drop of soap or some vinegar, and sometimes a few drops of essential oil, on surfaces that can tolerate a slightly damp cleaning. Lemon and grapefruit oils are good options, as they have cleansing qualities and not only make the house smell fresh but also help to clear energy stagnation.

Once you are done with decluttering, your home will feel more spacious and you will be energized to move on to the next building block, which is Using Colors. You may not be ready to repaint the entire home quite yet; nevertheless, this next chapter will change the way you look at color, inspire you to rethink your decorative color scheme, and perhaps even repaint a few rooms in the near future.

CHAPTER 4

Building Block Two—
Using Colors

t is always a joy to experience a beautiful color. I can easily spend an hour standing in front of the color racks in a paint store, totally immersed in all the different possibilities. Colors will not only create the kind of look we want to have in a space, but they will influence our emotions and mood. For example, blue will promote a feeling of relaxation; red and orange will be energizing; and pink can make us feel loved. This chapter will provide you with knowledge about energetic characteristics of colors, which will help you to decide how and where to implement them.

It is important to understand what we are trying to accomplish when deciding on new colors. Working with wall colors is one of the most effective ways to shift the energy of a space. A room's wall is a large area and greatly influences the room's energy. Once you read this chapter, review the colors in your home and see if you can feel their influence better. Perhaps something you've always felt but didn't know how to explain will become clearer.

Science and Research behind Color

Color is our perception of the narrow part of the electromagnetic spectrum called visible light. Different wavelengths in this spectrum correspond to different colors. The impact of different colors on our state of mind, emotions, and well-being is very different. Light and its influence on humans has been a subject of study since ancient times. There is evidence that in ancient Egypt there were healing solariums where light shone through colored gems such as rubies, sapphires, or emeralds. People were put into different colored chambers depending on the particular illness they came to heal. In ancient Greece in the city of Heliopolis, the city of the sun, a similar technique was used for therapeutic and spiritual purposes. In addition to colored light, every room had objects of the same color in it.

Starting four thousand years ago, those in the Far East used color to indicate cardinal directions (which essentially is Bagua), seasons, time of day, and the internal organs of the human body. Color is regarded as the vital force and energy that is able to heal.

The ideas behind the colors we use in feng shui come from an ancient observation-based method relating nature to human behavior. Currently, many forms of light therapy are still used, and environmental psychologists have done extensive research on how different colors influence our well-being and state of mind. The results of their research are being implemented by large hotels, spas, some hospitals, sports teams, and private companies. From my experience working with color, people report being happier, calmer, more creative, confident, and less stressed after repainting their room a more suitable color.

> *Some colors have light and expansive qualities, making a room feel larger and higher, while others have constrictive qualities and make the space feel smaller and tighter. Both qualities can be used to get the results we need. Some colors will exude joy and happiness, and some will make us feel balanced and grounded, while others are flat and unemotional.*

Fashion's Influence on Color

Room color is a big deal in interior design and feng shui. Some rules of color application will be similar, but feng shui incorporates much more detailed and precise color considerations for each room. While techniques are certainly helpful in steering us in the right general direction for our color choices, factors such as the nature of the room and the energy needs of the people, their aspirations, and their sense of aesthetics are important to consider and will help to further refine the color choices.

Interior design often follows color fashions. The paint colors being used now are very different than they were a few decades ago—even ten years ago. Right now, grays are popular. Ten or twenty years ago, beige was a favorite choice of interior designers, builders, and homeowners. Before that, people used more saturated colors such as reds, greens, blues, or yellows.

I understand the reason behind using neutral colors on walls. First, it's a big job to choose different colors for all the rooms. It's much easier to use one or two shades of a neutral beige or gray throughout the entire house. The second reason is that you want your furniture, rugs, and art to stand out. A neutral wall color definitely helps. But in so many houses, people end up with beige walls and beige couches and beige rugs—even beige couch pillows—with just a little variation in beige tones and a small dose of a few other colors. Guess what? A monochromatic environment doesn't have energy! Energy is created by contrast. This is why in these very neutral environments, people feel...neutral.

Unless you love working with color and consider it fun, you definitely don't need to repaint every room a different color to have a soulful home. If you prefer to choose a neutral color, choose a color that feels warm and light. The color must not feel flat, cold, or too dark. When I consult, I often ask to repaint one or two rooms—the ones that feel off or will have the biggest energetic impact. When people move into a new home or remodel, it is a great time to change most colors. This will help to bond with your new home and speed up a feeling of belonging.

I often get emails from clients with remarks like these: "I just finished painting the room, and wow! What a facelift! It looks awesome and so alive!" or "We started painting, and it feels like the house is transforming with every brushstroke" or "There is a feeling that the house has been injected with a beautiful, loving energy!"

Don't get me wrong. I don't mind using off-white or gray or any other neutral wall colors, especially if the architectural style of the house calls for it, but I make sure to compensate for it by using more of the other Elements to ensure the space is balanced and infused with positive feeling. Understanding the energetic qualities and characteristics of different colors will help to match a room and its color better, because different rooms are meant to be used for different activities.

Qualities and Meanings of Colors

To be able to use colors correctly and benefit from them, we need to understand the qualities of colors and how they may influence us. We also need to understand that each color has many hues, and if you go too far from the central color, the quality will not be the same as described here.

Red is a hot color. It is a stimulant. It evokes strong emotions. For some, it would invoke action and courage, for others excitement, passion, or motivation. There is plenty of data that suggests the most winning soccer teams and American college football teams wear red in their uniforms. For some people, red can be overwhelming and disturbing, for others it brings anger or irritation, and there are those who enjoy it. I suggest using red for walls in moderation and with caution. I never use it for an entire room, but sometimes it can work for a front door or a small accent wall. It is not appropriate to use in bedrooms. It is rare that people love or use pure red. It's usually some shade of red that people like. There are some absolutely beautiful and less intense variations of red. The Element of red color is yang Fire. Yang Fire means that it is a strong Fire.

Orange is less hot than red but is also a stimulating color. It is perceived as happy and joyful. It is associated with the sun and brings memories of happy vacations to exotic countries. It activates a feeling of optimism and confidence. Similar to red, I rarely use it for an entire room because it has a strong energy, but like red it is appropriate for accent walls. It is appropriate to use in dining rooms and dens or any area that needs to be energized. The Element of orange color is yang Fire.

Pink is a warm color. It has qualities of sweetness and kindness, love and happiness. It is a gentle color, and I like using some varieties of pink in bedrooms, especially if people want to bring some new and warm energy into their relationships. It is a color of love, after all! However, it has to be the right hue that harmonizes the heart and promotes happiness. The Element of pink color is yin Fire. Yin Fire means gentle or feminine Fire.

Yellow is a warm color. Similar to orange, yellow is associated with sunshine and happiness, but it is less intense than orange. Be cautious about using too bright shades of yellow because it might bring a sense of anxiety. It is warm, stimulating, and nourishing, so it supports digestion and mental activity, and it promotes socializing. People are attracted to its sun-like qualities. It is good to use yellow in kitchens or dining rooms where we have gatherings of people. It is not appropriate for an adult's bedroom, as it is an active color. The Element of yellow color is Earth. It can be either yin or yang, depending on the shade and level of saturation.

Tan or beige are warm colors. They have a calming influence and can produce a sense of warmth or comfort depending on the shade, but they don't produce much emotion, so it's no surprise they are considered neutral. The Element of tan or beige is yin Earth.

Green is in the middle of the visible color spectrum. It has balancing, nurturing, and even healing qualities. It is calming to the nervous system, most likely because trees and grass are green and we associate it with being in nature. These qualities are especially felt in warmer tones of greens. Brighter greens are more energizing and invoke the feelings of growth, expansion, abundance, and a sense of spring. Warm light greens are appropriate for family rooms, bedrooms, and home offices. The Element of green color is Wood, yin or yang, depending on the shade.

Blue is a cold color. It is calming to the nervous system. Lighter blue is associated with the expansiveness of the sky and darker blue reminds us of water. It evokes a state of tranquility and peace. The Element of pastel blue color is yin Water. A saturated blue can be yang Water. It is appropriate for bathrooms, some bedrooms, and some offices. Blue is not appropriate for kitchens or dining rooms.

Purple is warmer than blue, but colder than red. It is associated with depth, spirituality, prosperity, creativity, intuition, and beauty. It promotes a sense of calm, deep wisdom. Some shades of purple would be appropriate for an accent wall in a home office, and light shades might work for kids' bedrooms, but in general, purple is rarely used for walls. The Element of purple is yin Fire.

Gray is a cold color compared with other colors, but some shades of gray can feel on the warmer side. It is a neutral color and somewhat calming to the nervous system. Most shades of gray are perceived as neutral and do not evoke any emotional response. Light warm gray can be used for family rooms, dens, bedrooms, and transitional areas. The Element of gray color is yin Metal.

Black is a cold color. It is associated with power, authority, mystery, and depth. In essence, it is the absence of color that creates black. I do not recommend using black on walls. The Element of black is yin Water.

White is a cold color. It is the opposite of black. The presence of all the colors in the spectrum creates white. It has a clean and high vibration, but it doesn't have any emotion associated with it. The Element of white color is yang Metal. A good use of warmer white tones or so-called off-white colors is in hallways, stairways, and landings. In some rare cases in houses with special architectural details, a white color is appropriate for the entire house.

Now that you know the qualities of different colors, we can discuss general color application guidelines.

General Color Application Guidelines

Understanding the energy qualities of a particular color and knowing what experience you want to create in a particular space should guide your color choices. There will be more information on this in Part III as we go through each room of the house. Selecting colors is an individual process with no one-size-fits-all rules. Nevertheless, these general guidelines should be observed in most cases:

- ▶ Dark colors will make the room look smaller, and light colors will visually increase the size of the room. Use this according to your needs.
- ▶ If you use neutral wall colors, use more saturated colors in art, furniture, or rugs. The opposite is also true. If you paint the walls in brighter and bolder colors, choose furniture and rugs that are lighter and more neutral colors. This helps to create more vitality and balance between yin and yang aspects of the energy.
- ▶ If you have cathedral ceilings, slanted ceilings, or other angular architectural details, avoid dark or bright colors. The wall

color will create a strong contrast with the white ceiling and emphasize sharp angles and edges. It is an especially good rule to follow in bedrooms and family rooms, where you want to avoid sharp and unstable energy.

► Choose light colors in hallways and stairways. Colors that create a feeling of expansion are favorable there. A dark color makes narrow spaces feel even tighter, which creates the claustrophobic feeling of being in a tunnel.

► Use warmer and brighter colors in cold rooms and north-facing rooms where the sun does not shine.

► Do not use darker colors for the ceiling than what you use on the walls. It confuses our perception and disorients us on a subtle, subconscious level. Especially if the ceiling is low, painting it a lighter color than the walls will help to lift the space up visually.

► If you have normal height or low ceilings with lots of beams, it is better to paint the beams the same white color as the ceiling so they don't stand out as much. If the ceiling is high and beams do not feel oppressive or sharp and add some character to the design and architectural style, then you don't need to paint them. Use your judgment in how low the beams are and how they make you feel. If there are beams in an area where you don't spend much time, then worry less about their influence. If there are beams in the bedroom, above your work desk, or above your sofa, then address them.

► Remember, any color you see on a color swatch will look brighter on the wall.

▶ The same color will evoke different responses in different people.

In the next section, I will discuss some helpful personal trends that will help you to individualize your choices.

The Psychology behind Colors

I often see why people are attracted to certain colors and what guides their color choices in the home (besides fashion). People who have a lot of energy, project confidence, and have no trouble making decisions are often drawn to more bold and saturated colors including reds, purples, greens, and oranges whether it is wall colors or furniture and art colors. But there is a fine line, and going overboard with energizing colors can become overwhelming and produce restlessness and stress. People who have more gentle personalities tend to go with pastels or neutral schemes and can usually benefit from a bit of the opposite. Sometimes I suggest adding a stronger, brighter color to at least one room or wall to start shifting a client's energy toward more vibrancy and confidence. Choosing the right color can promote healing, hope, success, and optimism.

Your taste and style are important, and you may have some cultural inclinations toward certain colors, but you must also consider how the color makes you feel. Often, our choices come from the mind rather than from the heart. Environments that are created following your intuitive sense will be much more supportive than those that follow a design fashion, feng shui rules, or a forced theme.

Before I describe how different groups of people relate to color, let's consider two scenarios.

When you were growing up, you spent many happy days at your grandmother's house. She had a special room for you where she would come and read you stories and spend time with you before you fell asleep. The room was painted in an aqua blue color. Now, you might have lost your conscious connection to why you love aqua blue, but it makes you happy and comforted when you see it.

Here is another scenario. You had a difficult childhood. Your parents were fighting and finally divorced when you were eight years old. There were always arguments and feelings of unease at the dinner table. The kitchen and the adjacent eating area were painted green. It is quite probable that now you feel very uncomfortable in green rooms.

Some scenarios are not as obvious as these two, but, nevertheless, our subconscious stores a lot of these associations between the colors of our environments and our emotions. Unless we discharge the negative emotion behind a certain color or design style, it would be wise not to use it.

Color is an electromagnetic energy, and we are complex beings. Needless to say, colors affect us differently. These guidelines should be helpful in narrowing down your color choices.

I invite you to look at a color and see how it makes you feel. If you have a positive reaction and feel expanded, uplifted, calm, relaxed, excited, or joyful, this color is likely going to work for you. If you feel sad, irritated, repelled, or your energy contracts, this is not a good color choice for you. You don't have to analyze why it is happening or how it works; just follow your inner guidance. It is best if this feeling comes not from your thinking mind but from your heart, your gut, or your intuitive self.

It's actually very simple. You either like it, don't like it, or it is neutral. Neutral is not too bad in this case. If it happens to be one of the colors I recommend further along in this book, it might be worth trying. I use this technique with my clients when we work on a color scheme, and I typically offer a few choices then wait for the best response. Sometimes the response is neutral, but I know it is a good choice because I know the energy characteristics of the color and can predict how it will influence people in the space. In that case, I ask the client to give it a try and let me know how it feels in a few months. In that scenario, 99 percent of people say they love it as soon as they see it and feel it in the room.

Lorena's Story

My client's story can illustrate how one's energy would benefit from utilizing the right Elements and colors. I met Lorena when she had separated from her longtime partner and was renting a small apartment. She was a talented musician and singer but could not make a reasonable living doing what she loved. She was struggling and didn't know how to get out of this difficult situation.

We worked on having clarity for her career and relationships and bringing in more income in the meantime. She was an immigrant from Brazil, and, as we talked, we discovered that she missed the warm, sunny, and ardent environment where she grew up. She was naturally drawn to bright and bold colors, rich paintings, and beautiful things. She realized she was holding back and suppressing her desire for those things because she thought she could not afford them. Although we could not paint the entire room in a rental apartment, she got inspired and said she'd paint one wall and would paint it white again when she moved out. The color that made her heart sing was earthy orange.

We found creative ways to make her environment reflect who she was without spending too much money. Surrounded by the colors and things that supported her energy, Lorena became more confident and discovered that she is stronger and braver than she thought. While still doing her music gigs, she went back to school and got a degree in healthcare administration.

Within six months of our initial meeting, she reconnected again with her partner, John, as it became clear to them that they were good for each other. I consulted with them about their apartment when they reconciled. And when John got a raise at work, which enabled them to buy a house, I helped them choose a home with good feng shui properties.

Lorena was already an experienced designer, and with some direction from me, she created an amazing, colorful, and magical environment for her and John. I revisit their home every year to keep tweaking and fine-tuning the environment to support their unfolding story of personal and professional growth. I love spending time in their home because everything emanates love, joy, and passion. For the last five years, John has gotten multiple raises, so they bought an investment property, and last year, Lorena went back to school again to get her master's degree in administration. Every year she feels more fulfilled, happy, and confident.

In the next section, we will discuss how different colors can promote different aspects of your well-being.

Using Color for
Balance and Well-Being

▶ If you are a high-powered alpha personality and, for the most part, feel robust and strong, you are probably attracted to bold and bright colors such as red, orange, yellow, saturated green, or blue. Most likely they are great for you, but make sure you don't use them throughout the entire house. Tone these colors down a bit in some rooms because you, too, need to be able to relax at times.

▶ If you are a shy and gentle person, bright and bold colors most likely would be too much stimulation and would overload your reserved demeanor. You would benefit from soft, uplifting, pastel colors such as gentle pinks, gentle greens, creams, and soft yellows. If it feels right, you may give it a try and paint one room or one accent wall using a bold color just for fun, or get a large and vibrant piece of art. It might give you just the right amount of stimulation and inspiration.

▶ If you tire easily, feel stressed, or are under a lot of pressure, I would suggest not using bright and bold colors. You would benefit from more greens, blues, or grays. This will help you to relax yet feel supported and connected with nature and your own essence. Make sure to include some muted yellow or gentle pink to nourish you in a balanced way.

▶ If you are depressed or sad, use warm colors: pinks, greens, and yellows especially, and experiment with bringing some brighter, bolder colors into one or two rooms.

- ▶ If you have difficulty concentrating, you would benefit from less stimulation and a calmer color scheme, and not too many different wall colors all together. Blue will help you relax, and soft gray or tan will ground you.
- ▶ If you get angry easily, do not use bold red, orange, or green colors. Yellow, blue, or pastel green will help you feel more balanced.
- ▶ If you are strong minded, too serious, and a perfectionist, most likely you are attracted to fashion-dictated colors, such as gray or another neutral color scheme. You may find joy by letting go a bit and introducing a different color in one or two rooms, just for fun. Trust me, it is worth giving it a try.
- ▶ If you feel stagnant and want change, use something new you haven't used before. Try greens, purples, hot pinks, or even orange colors.
- ▶ If you are in a new phase of creativity, implementing new ideas, or starting a new business, green is great for infusing your new ideas with a rising type of energy. Also, some amount of red, orange, purple, or pink will give you a needed boost and power you up.
- ▶ If you want to attract new friends and strengthen your social status, yellow can help you with this.
- ▶ If you want to infuse your current relationship with a new energy, or attract a new partner, pink will nourish your heart and help to bring the vibration of love into your home.
- ▶ If you feel burnt out or simply want to be able to relax and rejuvenate, blues are good for you at this time.

Colors for Specific Directions or the Bagua

In Chapter 2, we talked about different aspects of the Bagua and the reason behind using specific colors for eight directions or sectors of the Bagua.

The important thing to know is that it is not necessary to use the Bagua-suggested colors for your wall colors. More goes into creating a beautiful and supportive environment than just applying the Bagua-suggested colors mechanically, especially to the walls. That is why I am placing this section at the end of the chapter on colors.

Although we will discuss the Bagua colors in this section, you will see that after you apply the Bagua to your floor plan, most of the colors will not be appropriate for the type of room or your personality type, or you will simply not like the color. Only after you consider these factors can you look at the Bagua color chart and see if the colors can be implemented for the walls, or if they would be better used in art, furniture, and accessories.

Besides colors, the Bagua's Five Elements can be implemented in the materials and shapes of the furniture, accessories, rugs, accent pillows, art, and plants, i.e., all the elements of design.

Choosing a room color is an organic process, and it involves an understanding of the nature of the room and how the room is being used. We will go over this and consider every room in detail in Part III. Sometimes it is appropriate and beautiful to have one (or very few) accent walls painted in rich, saturated colors. The wall becomes art on its own. For the entire room, it is often best to use lighter and more neutral colors.

It's useful to get familiar with the Bagua colors so you don't make the mistake of undermining the energy of the room. For example, painting your southeastern room, which relates to prosperity and wealth, in gray would be a mistake because the strongest Element of the room will be Metal. Metal will reduce the Wood, and Wood relates to the growth of your prosperity.

Here is the list of the directions, along with the colors that are best aligned with the energy of each direction. As I mentioned before, you don't need to implement these colors onto your room's walls unless it works well for the room, fits your personality, and you like the color. These colors can be added as accent colors to the rugs, art, sofa pillows, and accessories.

East represents growth, family, and health. The Elements of the east are Wood and Water. The colors of the east are lighter and brighter greens, blues, and turquoise. It is great if you choose shades that have uplifting and expansive qualities. Brighter greens and turquoise are appropriate for children's rooms, bathrooms, the front door, or a special accent wall in the home office or family room.

Southeast is associated with prosperity and wealth. The Elements of the southeast are Wood and Water, and the colors are green and blue. Softer or darker greens are best in the southeast, although any greens that speak to you are quite appropriate. Purple can also be used in the southeast. Purple has a high vibrational frequency and is considered a color of prosperity in classical Chinese feng shui. Which color is most appropriate depends on the room. Soft greens or blues are great for a special accent wall. Purple would make the front door look special or the powder room look rich and interesting.

South represents fame and reputation. The Element of the south is Fire, and Fire is strengthened by Wood. Red, orange, pink, and bright greens are appropriate colors in southern rooms according to the Bagua. But, practically speaking, the southern room is the warmest room in the house, and using a hot color for the entire room would create too much heat and be overwhelming for most people, especially if there are large windows and great exposure to sunlight. I rarely use reds and oranges on walls, especially in hot southern rooms, but I sometimes use them for accent colors to nurture a feeling of joy. If you crave something red, choose raspberry, magenta, or fuchsia. They are delicious colors and can be used for accents and the front door. There will be more information on colors for the front door in Chapter 10.

Southwest represents relationships and the mother of the family. The Element of the southwest is Earth, and Earth is supported by Fire. Fire colors are red, hot pink, and orange, and the colors of the Earth are yellow, tan, and terra-cotta. I love using soft pink or coral colors on southwest walls. Sometimes, a small amount of red would be appropriate too, but it could also bring too much tension into relationships. Pinks or corals are softer and quite perfect there. In some areas, hot pink would work well for an accent wall or in a piece of art. Corals or yellows would go well with the active nature of a dining room or add warmth to a bathroom. Certain shades of pink would bring a heartfelt feeling and joy to a bedroom. Yellows work nicely in the kitchen. Tan can be used in the family room or dining room.

West is associated with children and creativity. The Element of the west is Metal, and Metal is supported by Earth. The Metal colors are white, gray, silver, and gold. Silver and gold colors might work best in textured wallpaper. They will make the room look and feel dressy and special. Earth colors are yellow and tan. The Earth Element could be nicely and organically implemented on walls using a natural, woven grass cloth, which is textured and will bring a feeling of connection to the natural world. Golds or grass cloth would also work nicely in the dining room. Beige, light gray, or white would work well in hallways or stairways.

Northwest represents helpful people and the father of the family. The Element of the northwest is Metal, and Metal is supported by Earth. All the Metal and Earth colors are appropriate in this area, but the energy of the northwest is very different from the playful and joyful west. More formal variations of silver and gold colors would be good to accentuate this aspect. A dressy golden or silver wallpaper accent wall might be quite appropriate for a special northwestern room.

North is the direction of career. The Element of the north is Water, and Metal supports Water. According to the Bagua, appropriate colors for northern rooms are blue, white, gray, and silver. The important thing that people overlook here is that the north is colder and darker, as there is no direct sun. The use of cold colors such as blue, white, or gray for the walls will accentuate the coldness of the room, and, as a result, you will not want to spend time there. I use only warm-toned, light pastels on the walls. Sometimes, but very rarely, a warmer variation of saturated and vivid blue might work in the north—an accent wall or front door—especially if blue is your favorite color. Pastel colors are appropriate in most of the rooms.

Northeast is the direction of knowledge and self-development. The Element of the northeast is Earth. The nature of the northeast is such that greens, blues, and aqua are appropriate here, along with the expected tans and yellows. Because the northeastern room will not have any sun during the day except early in the morning, it is best if the color is warm and pastel. Pastel colors are appropriate in most northeastern rooms.

After reading this chapter on color, you may want to assess your home's colors—if you haven't already done so—and see how they make you feel. You might be able to understand more why you made those choices for your walls, furniture, art, and accessories. If you are happy with your choices, then there is no need to do anything, but if you feel there is room for improvement, go for it!

If you come up with more than one color choice, choose the one that gives you a stronger sense of confidence or joy. If you are still unsure, paint part of the wall or a white board with your top choices and let yourself feel them. If you look at the color and have an uplifting or expanding sensation in your chest, a comforting feeling in your belly, or a spark of joy in your heart, this is your color. The first sensation is usually right, but you may want to come back to this exercise a few more times at different times of the day with different lighting. And if you prefer all the walls be neutral, you may get a few ideas from this color guide for the colors of your rugs, furniture, art, and accessories, which are the next building blocks we'll turn our attention to.

As a bonus, my e-book *Interior Color, Room by Room Guide* is available to you at no charge on my website, www.nataliakaylin.com. It has actual Benjamin Moore samples of all the room colors, along with color photos of the rooms. I created it as a complementary interior color guide for those who would like to dive deeper and use actual color samples. In addition, there is a Projects section on my website with many photos of beautiful interiors that I worked on.

CHAPTER 5

Building Block Three— Furniture

F urniture is naturally our next big building block and an important foundation for creating an environment. With so many choices out there, it's often hard to navigate.

> *In reality, furniture and all the material items in our home are energy that is condensed into a form, shape, color, and texture. As with any other kind of energy, furniture can be complementary to our own energy—or not so much.*

A simple example is a good-looking but uncomfortable sofa or a desk that is too small for you or a mattress that is either too hard or too soft. Furniture that is comfortable and pleasing to our senses and compatible with our size and the size of the room will contribute to creating a feeling of nourishment, relaxation, balance, and satisfaction. Furniture that is the wrong size, too hard, too soft, old, or partially broken is going bring emotions such as *I am not good enough, I don't deserve something better, I don't have enough money, I've made a wrong choice and now have to stick with it, etc.* It is not necessarily the loud, straightforward thinking, but rather, the underlying, unspoken, subtle messages in our subconscious mind that contribute to being stuck in a negative story. You may want to make some assessments right now, allowing yourself to feel the emotional responses while you are going from piece to piece.

I see and hear from many clients about "mistakes they've made" and "now they have to live with those mistakes." I personally think all mistakes are valuable and provide lessons.

> *The furniture mistakes tend to be expensive ones. Nevertheless, you don't have to keep living with your mistakes! And to be completely correct here, we grow out of yesterday's choices—sometimes fast—and our taste keeps developing and refining.*

My client Anne told me that she has hated her new couch for over a year now. It was supposed to be a comfortable one for her TV room where she and her husband could snuggle together to watch movies a few times a week. But the couch was uncomfortable to the point that she could not relax and enjoy it. Over time, she found that she and her husband spent more and more time in their offices instead of hanging out together. If this had continued much longer, new habits would be formed, and the closeness in their relationship would suffer. Anne confirmed my thoughts and decided that it was worth getting a new couch.

The flow of energy is equally important. A flow is created from the placement of all the furniture pieces, especially big ones, such as a sofa, a dining room table, or a bed. Feng shui is often referred to as an art of placement. We want to make sure the energy flows freely in a meandering kind of way, that it is not stuck, obstructed, or moving too fast.

An example of fast-moving energy is when furniture pieces are placed in straight lines rather than an organic, meandering way. There is a sense of warmth and relaxed closeness in semiround sitting areas where energy can gather around the focal point. There will be more on this in Section III when we work on individual rooms.

If the furniture pieces are well-proportioned with the room and are well-placed, allowing easy access to everything, it will contribute to a sense of harmony and well-being in the room. If there are too many pieces of furniture in one room or they are placed incorrectly, the flow will be compromised. If the room is too small and we use oversized pieces, it will not look or feel right, and the energy will feel stuck.

When people move from a smaller house to a bigger house or downsize, they often bring their furniture with them. While it looked and felt good in the previous home, it may feel out of place in the new space. When people move to larger homes, sometimes they bring their small-sized tables and sofas, and it looks like the furniture pieces are floating in the space. In addition to not looking right, this creates a sense of being ungrounded. The furniture size must be proportional to the size of the room.

Clair's Story

I remember a client named Clair who was single for some time and really wanted to engage in a new relationship. During my tour of her home, I found a few interesting things. First, the house felt pretty cluttered. There were too many pieces of mismatched furniture everywhere, especially smaller items like bookshelves, side tables, chairs, and lamps. They were different styles, ages, and colors, which created a sense of disharmony and being stuck. The piece that particularly got my attention was an old, not-so-great-looking desk in the family room. Clair told me that she had inherited it from her grandmother, and the desk was broken. She had planned to fix it and refurbish it for over a decade now. When I asked how she felt about the desk, she admitted that along with feeling love for her grandmother, the desk brought a feeling of sadness, and the fact that she procrastinated about fixing it irritated her.

I kept digging deeper and asked a few questions about her grandmother. It turned out that her grandmother was a strong woman who was also single, and Clair remembered her often being sad. You see the similarity here. Additionally, Clair had trouble managing her weight and generally felt stuck. Upon completing my findings inside her house, I also discovered that there was a large dead tree in the southwestern part of her yard.

The interesting thing was that both the desk and the tree were at the southwestern part of the house. If you remember, in the Bagua section we talked about how the southwest relates to female health and relationships. Overgrown shrubs blocked both the main entrance to her home and the mudroom entrance. After we discussed these findings along with some others, Clair worked hard on reducing the clutter and opening up the flow of energy inside and outside her home. She hired someone to remove the dead tree. She also got an estimate for fixing her grandmother's desk and decided it was not worth it, so she let go of it. She did other things in the house aimed at helping her bring a feeling of love, prosperity, well-being, and joy. A few months later, I got an email from her: "Three weeks after I implemented all of your suggestions, I joined Match for the first time, and I met an amazing man within four days! We are connected in mind, body, spirit, and soul. It's incredible." She sounded like a completely different person, bursting with joy and confidence. She lost weight, and her business picked up so much that she had to hire an assistant.

Antique Furniture

Antique furniture deserves a special mention. By definition, it is old and some of it has seen a few owners. Every time I see antique furniture pieces in my clients' homes, I tune into them. More than half of it doesn't feel good. Furniture absorbs people's emotions, and with time there is an accumulation of emotions and other people's energy. Sometimes, if a piece was in the bedroom of someone who was sick for a while or died, the piece has absorbed the energy and emotion of sickness as well.

If a piece of antique furniture doesn't feel good, I ask where it came from. If it came from the family and has a positive meaning, then it is worth keeping. If it needs refurbishing or fixing, do it sooner rather than later. If it came from a yard sale or antique store, keep in mind that there is no way to know the circumstances surrounding the piece. If you love the piece and it has some value to you, energy clearing may help to reset its energy, but I have to admit it doesn't always work—even if I do it myself.

Sometimes the best thing to do is to let go of the piece. Keep in mind that all antique furniture is yin by nature. In other words, its energy is on the low side. If you are a person whose personal energy is on the low side, then filling your house with antiques is definitely not great for you.

Once I worked with a couple whose hobby was to hunt yard sales and every antique store in the area for special pieces. They lived in a two-hundred-year-old, antique kind of house and thought it was interesting to submerge themselves in the past. It was a great learning experience for me. When I saw the house for the first time, it felt more like a museum than a real home. The space was quite dark, and the rooms were quite small. The house's energy felt incredibly low. Each piece had a story and emotions in it, and it felt almost like a mist surrounded those numerous pieces and the entire house.

The couple hired me because they had some variety of health and relationship issues and felt it had something to do with the house. I told them how I perceived their antiques, and they agreed to let go of some of the most toxic pieces, which we identified together. After they did that, they felt better. They also realized they were not living their real lives because they had become consumed by their collection. I heard from them about a year after our initial consultation, when they hired me to consult on their new home. They had taken my advice to heart, bought a new home, sold all (!) of their antiques, and bought new contemporary furniture that matched their energy needs much better. It was especially great for the woman, who sparkled with joy and enthusiasm. Ever since then, I keep my eye on antiques in my clients' homes to make sure they are not draining or diminishing the energy. You can simply tune in and see for yourself how a certain piece makes you feel.

Yin/Yang and the Five Elements in Furniture

The presence of opposite shapes, colors, materials, and heights helps to create a sense of harmony, comfort, and most of all, balance. The most balanced spaces will have a similar amount of objects with yin and yang energies.

Yin furniture: older, darker, antique furniture, low furniture like sofas (especially darker ones), coffee tables (especially round or oval shaped), beds, carpet, flooring, rugs (especially dark colored), ottomans; green, blue, gray, or beige furniture.

Yang furniture: new furniture, tall furniture like bookshelves, leather and square-shaped ottomans, hard-surface floors like hardwood or tile, brightly colored rugs; red, orange, yellow, or white furniture.

It is tricky to identify the **Five Elements** in furniture because often there is a mix of two or even three different Elements. Unless it is obvious, just don't worry too much about it, and if you need to balance the Five Elements, you can use colors, plants, accessories, and art in whichever Elements are more prominent.

The following classifications might be useful.

In general, furniture such as sofas, chairs, and ottomans are of Earth Element. Their shapes are mostly rectangular and square, and often their color is earthy tones: tan, beige, or chocolate. Sofas and chairs hold us while we relax in them, which is a nourishing attribute of Earth Element. They can combine two Elements. For example, a red sofa consists of Fire and Earth Elements, and a white sofa will be Earth and Metal Elements.

Beds are Water Element, but if they are made of wood and with a wood headboard, Wood Element will be present too.

Rugs are Water Element in general, but brightly colored rugs with geometric patterns can bring in other Elements.

Wooden bookshelves, cabinets, and some desks are Wood Elements, but only when they are new and unpainted. When they age, the energy of Wood is not strong anymore.

Floor lamps and table lamps are Fire Elements, which brings us to the next chapter.

CHAPTER 6

Building Block Four— Lighting

Lighting is often an underestimated and overlooked aspect of living and furnishing. The right amount and the right kind of lighting is not only a necessity or aesthetic feature but will create a big difference in your well-being. Interior design considers three types of basic lighting in a home: general or ambient lighting, task lighting, and accent lighting.

Ambient lighting is needed to create an overall uniform illumination of the room. It is natural light that comes through the windows or light created by recessed lighting or tall torchiere lamps. In modern, high-end homes, cove lighting is being used more often now. It is a form of indirect lighting built into ledges, recesses, or valances in a ceiling or high on the walls of a room. Because the light bounces off the ceiling, it provides uniform lighting that closely resembles natural lighting.

Task lighting is used to illuminate a specific area where a certain function can be performed. This includes specifically positioned recessed lights or pendants above kitchen countertops, a chandelier above the dining room table, or an office desk lamp.

Accent lighting is used to draw our attention to a particular object in the room such as a piece of art or family photos. Wall sconces, track lighting, and cove lighting can be used for this. Accent lighting in the form of a directed source light is also used in landscaping to illuminate a statue, water feature, flag, or beautiful tree.

Yin/Yang and the Five Elements in Lighting

All types of lighting are of Fire Element.

Yin and yang are always seen in relation to each other. In relation to other objects, lighting is almost always yang. By comparing different types of lighting with each other, we can categorize them into yin or yang.

Examples of yin types of lighting are a table lamp or a low-wattage ceiling pendant.

Examples of yang types of lighting are large chandeliers, especially crystal ones, tall torchiere lamps, or recessed lighting.

Both yin and yang types should be utilized throughout the home to fulfill various functions and create a different atmosphere and mood in different spaces. While yin types are better for relaxation or reading, yang lighting is used to expand and elevate the energy, enliven the space, and uplift the mood.

Increasing Natural Lighting

Almost everyone notices that natural light reduces fatigue and is better for our mood.

> *Studies show that natural light helps to regulate our hormones and circadian rhythms, therefore positively influencing our health, productivity, and happiness.*

Using softer and warmer lighting in the evening does not disrupt the production of melatonin, which is sometimes called the sleeping hormone. Research even suggests that red, green, and yellow hues will stimulate melatonin production, while bright, cold white and blue lights in the evening may disrupt melatonin and stimulate the production of serotonin instead.

Whenever possible, try to maximize the use of natural light:

- On overcast days, choose the lighting that is closest to natural sunlight. Our circadian rhythms are regulated better if we are exposed to the colder or bluer part of the spectrum during the day and the warmer, yellow part of the spectrum at night.
- Open the shades and curtains fully during the day. I sometimes notice that people leave the shades down during the day, and the energy in the room gradually becomes lower and more stagnant with time. The only way I can explain this is that the sun not only uplifts the energy of the space when it shines into the room, but somehow charges it up. Hence, northern rooms always feel more yin than southern rooms where the sun shines directly into the room. A southern room has a more vibrant feel to it, even in the evening or when it is overcast.

▶ To me, curtains are overrated and are used less and less in newer homes. They can add something beautiful and special to the design and feel of the house if they are done by a professional designer who has great taste, and you are willing to pay a few thousand dollars for them. Most often curtains are not so special, and they tend to block more natural light than window shades because of the extra bulk. Shades do not block natural light during the day, and they can be moved up or down for privacy and maximum light. Shades will also help preserve heat and, therefore, lower your heating bill during the winter. If you want to save a significant amount of money, you can measure the window frame yourself and order them online. Any online store that sells shades will have clear instructions on how to take measurements. You can get samples of the shades mailed to you to see the color and texture before you order. If this seems like too much, and you don't have a budget to work with a designer, you can also hire a professional installer from Home Depot or Lowe's to do the measurements for you.

▶ If you work from home and have a choice, try to work from a room that has more natural lighting. For example, for your home office choose a room with windows or part of any other appropriate room with windows. See more about home office lighting and desk placement in Chapter 18.

Lighting is, in many ways, responsible for creating the appropriate atmosphere in various parts of a home.

Chandeliers are a great way to create a statement and bring beauty for larger homes and homes with higher ceilings. Ceiling pendants and torchiere lamps are good for uplifting the energy in homes with normal or lower ceilings. Crystal chandeliers and pendants are fun, but they are considered a more classical option. If your design style is more contemporary, there are other beautiful and more contemporary options like cascading raindrop glass bubbles or hand-blown patterned glass cups that will work just as well. Cascading chandeliers are especially good for a two-story open entryway staircase because they can be longer and fill the area better.

Table lamps serve well for creating an intimate and relaxing atmosphere in the evening. A warmer choice of LED is best to use for table lamps. A warmer, softer pendant or chandelier light is also preferable for dining in the evenings. After all, for most of history humans dined either around the fire or by candlelight.

There are so many spectacular choices out there, especially online. It's easier if you can find what you want in the store, but stores do not have as many options on display compared to what you can find online. If you buy lighting online, make sure to read all the specifications and measurements very carefully so you know exactly the size and wattage you are getting.

Chandeliers, pendants, floor lamps, and table lamps can absolutely be considered an art item in addition to their functional use. In the next section, let's immerse ourselves in the process of creating beauty and emotion with art.

CHAPTER 7

Building Block Five—Art

Often art is the easiest and the most fun layer to work with. A good piece of art or a photograph often carries an emotion or a feeling. This is why art is an important element in rewriting our story. A good art choice can make a room feel either alive and vibrant or peaceful and tranquil. It can be personalized further by bringing a feeling of hope, joy, love, confidence, or whatever feeling you want to have present in your life at this time.

Our art choices not only express our creativity, inspiration, or passion, but can tell a lot about us. If we are sad and depressed, we will probably be drawn to art with darker tones and sad emotions. Images that emanate similar emotions to what we experience will resonate with our state of mind. It's like we see the world through our sadness. Often sadness is represented by autumn motifs with trees losing leaves, winter with bare trees, cloudy skies, or dark and stormy waters.

My clients' story is a good demonstration of how art can influence our state of mind.

Robert and Dawn's Story

I worked with Robert and Dawn a long time ago, but their story is something I will never forget. At the time of our session, they had been together for almost four years and cared for each other a great deal, but Robert suffered from alcoholism and depression, and for periods of time he could not work and contribute to their family's finances. Dawn was overly stretched, providing for both of them. What stood out to me during our consultation was that some rooms were painted in cold gray and dark blue, and the art was either black and white or had sad and dark motifs. I remember one particularly large painting in their family room. It was an original masterpiece, but it depicted a dark and stormy ocean. Robert confirmed that the art came with him and had been with him for a while. He considered himself a sophisticated art collector. I remembered my teacher, Roger Green, saying that it is a classical case that people who have a tendency toward depression and alcoholism are drawn to images of dark water.

According to the Five Elements principle, we needed to bring Wood and Fire Elements into the house to drain and exhaust the Water, which was in excess. I advised changing the colors of those particularly dark rooms, replacing some art pieces, and bringing in plants. Robert wrote that he sold some of his art, and they had a great time together picking new pieces with green, red, purple, and orange colors and happier motifs. They also repainted two particularly dark rooms—the entrance and Robert's office—with lighter and warmer colors and bought a few large plants to reduce the Water Element more. Their environment became much more uplifting and vibrant. I heard from Dawn again after six months. Robert wasn't drinking anymore, their business had picked up, and Dawn shared that they decided to start a family. I remember many beautiful client stories, but Robert and Dawn's story touches my heart in a special way.

If we are happy, energetic, and successful, we will be drawn to pieces with bright colors, such as red, orange, purple, blue, or green. If we are financially or emotionally insecure, we will choose smaller art pieces, and if we are confident, we will choose large pieces with open spaces in them.

Often, single women have one or a few pictures of individual women throughout the house. Even though they would love to be in a relationship, they lock themselves into a state of mind where they are reminded that they are single, which becomes familiar territory and comfortable over time. Some of these psychological correspondences are also described in Chapter 1, in the section "Identifying Blockages."

The most fascinating thing is that images can change our state of mind. During the last few decades, numerous studies have confirmed this, although it was already known to feng shui masters centuries ago. A large percentage of our brain is dedicated to image processing, and it happens very fast, in a fraction of a second. The studies concluded that, for the brain, it doesn't matter whether it is a real thing or an image. We get similar responses.

A beautiful image of a beach and water, especially if the image reminds you of your favorite vacation spot or a place you want to go, can bring instant happiness and relaxation. The stronger the emotional response you get from the image, the better it will work for you. If an image of a house on the beach represents your wealth dream and you place it in an area where you see it often, it will serve as a subconscious reminder of what you want. And it is easy and inexpensive to do with so many beautiful choices on the web from Art.com, GreatBigCanvas.com, or any other art site.

> *I have observed hundreds of cases of people's lives changing because they surrounded themselves with art that represented how they want to feel rather than how they actually feel in the present or felt in the past.*

I also encourage people to use their own photos. Everyone has thousands of beautiful photos that can easily be transformed into a piece of art that you and your family will enjoy. It will work wonders for you because you already have an emotional connection to the image. Make sure you were happy at the time the photo was taken. This matters a great deal. Consciously or subconsciously, your mind will remember the emotion you had at that moment. If there was any tension when the photo was taken, this information is stored in your subconscious mind and will influence you every time you see the photo. There are many easy and inexpensive options online to turn your photos into wall hangings. My favorite choice is Easy Canvas Print. In my home, we have three photos 24" x 40" over my family room's couch and four photos in my husband's office from our travels. I prefer my own photos in my family room because they have lots of great memories, they are beautiful, and they're lots of fun. I change my photos once every four to six years to bring fresh energy.

I recommend looking at all the art pieces in your home and allowing yourself to feel the emotional responses and the energy they invoke in you. Typically, the first response is the most accurate one, but if you are not sure, ask yourself the following questions when you stand in front of a particular piece of art or a photograph. Allow yourself to feel a sensation in your body, or in your energy field, rather than in your thinking mind.

- ▸ Does my energy expand, or does it shrink?
- ▸ Do I feel a pleasant or unpleasant sensation in my heart, my belly, or my throat?
- ▸ Do I feel joy or sadness?
- ▸ Does it feel like the old me or the new me?
- ▸ Does it make me feel the way I want to feel or not?

I hope you've already gone through the exercise in Chapter 1 "Identifying What You Want" and determined what new things you want to bring into your life. If you have not yet, now it is a good time to do so.

All these choices should be individual; here are a few ideas that might help you move in the right direction:

- ▸ Many people will associate a feeling of peace, tranquility, and relaxation with images of water such as beautiful, sunlit, calm ocean waters with blue or aqua colors, beaches, sunsets or sunrises on the ocean, houses on the beach, or lakes. For some people it might be pictures of meadows, vineyards, and gentle rolling hills. The colors should not be too bright and rich but also not very washed-out either. If it is too pastel or uniform, the picture may not have enough energy to carry an emotion. Not always, though; sometimes it is very refined and subtle.

▶ A feeling of freedom, expansion, and excitement can be depicted by fast-moving sailboats or ocean regattas, running horses, and exotic travel destinations.

▶ A feeling of abundance and wealth may come from all of the above plus pictures of lush green trees, plants, flowers, and fruits. The colors in the wealth-related images should be relatively rich and bright rather than subtle.

▶ A feeling of passionate love can be depicted by two running horses, a dancing couple, or rich red or hot pink colors.

▶ A feeling of tender love can be associated with two sensual flowers, two gentle animals, and light pastel colors (especially pinks).

▶ A feeling of romantic love is usually depicted in pictures of a couple walking on the beach or the streets of Paris in spring.

▶ A feeling of joy and happiness may come with sunshine, spring or summer, beaches, flowers, birds, or any other animals you are connected with or special places that you've visited.

▶ A feeling of being at a spa, relaxation, and rejuvenation can be created with images of orchids—especially white or pink ones—as well as seashells or pebbles.

Yin/Yang and the Five Elements in Art

Yin art: small-sized pieces; pastel, soothing, relaxing landscapes; images of women; fall and winter themes; black-and-white photos; refined art; dark and sad images.

Yang art: large pieces; brightly colored pieces; images that depict sharp features, angles, or many straight lines and geometrical shapes; dynamic or exciting images; images of men; images of rock stars (men and women).

Some areas of the home will benefit from yin artwork, and some will do better with yang artwork.

The Five Elements: Water, Wood, Fire, Earth, and Metal can easily and beautifully be implemented with art.

Wood Element

Wood Element is used in places where the energy needs to be uplifted. Wood is about growth. The tree is a growing, living thing nourished by water, sun, and nutrients from the earth just like our prosperity has to be nourished by our hard work, our right attitudes, and actions. Wood Element is associated with prosperity—we definitely want that energy to grow and expand. It is the vertical quality of the Wood that we are interested in. Therefore, images of trees such as aspens or bamboo are best if you need to bring a strong Wood Element.

Fire Element

Fire Element is great for expressing positive emotions such as joy, love, passion, happiness, fulfillment, and excitement, as well as the aspect of reputation. Using art with red, orange, and pink colors helps to express those emotions. Reds will feel like strong yang Fire and pinks will be gentle or yin Fire. Examples of Fire Element art are images of horses, exotic feline animals, exotic birds, and red, pink, purple, or orange flowers. Posters of sports and famous sports figures, rock and roll concerts and famous musicians, and red sports cars belong to Fire Element as well.

Earth Element

Earth Element is best depicted in photos or paintings of hills, meadows, and mountains. There might be some trees in the picture, but land should be more prominent than trees. If you choose a picture of mountains, make sure there are no sharp peaks; it is best if the picture has warm and nourishing qualities in it, rather than sharp and cold. The predominant colors should be yellow, brown, and tan, although the addition of some orange, purple, and green in the picture would make it more vibrant and joyful. Hills and vineyards of Tuscany, lavender fields of Southern France, or meadows and fields of flowers are a perfect example of the beautiful Earth Element in art.

Metal Element

Examples of Metal Element in art are metal statues, figurines, and wall art. White color and round shapes are considered to be Metal Element as well, but the easiest way to implement Metal Element is to use things made of metal, which includes items that are not metal but are painted with metallic paint (although, it is not as strong a representation as things made of metal).

Water Element

Water Element is used in feng shui pretty extensively, as water is associated with prosperity, relaxation, rejuvenation, adventure, and vacation —in other words, all the good things in life. Ships and sailboats are associated with wealth, but use them only if you like boats and sailing or it is something you want in the future. Otherwise a beautiful ocean, lake, or fish pond is a better choice because you may have a better connection with it. The ocean is considered to be yang Water, while a lake or pond is yin Water. A fast-moving river is yang Water, and a slow-moving stream is yin Water.

The process of finding the right piece of art is very individual. I am no art expert, but I am sensitive to art. Some images evoke much stronger emotional responses than others. Search until something "clicks." It should feel good, look good, and fit well with your environment and style. If you get two or three images that have a similar feeling, see which one goes best with your colors and furniture. But it doesn't have to be a perfect fit. Sometimes it is totally fine if there is some imperfection, unless you know it is going to bother you.

Remember that you might have something in your own photo collection that will work well, and if you can't find anything that satisfies you at this time, then you may get inspired to take some photos or even paint it. Some of my clients did just that and got great results, plus they opened up more to their creativity. I remember one client, in particular, who could not find the right art piece that would project the feeling she wanted to be surrounded with in her home—so she created it. After our session, she started to paint for her home. The process of painting gave her a lot of inspiration, so she didn't want to stop and then started to sell her paintings in galleries on the East and West Coasts. Other options, of course, are to visit galleries or commission an artist to paint it for you.

Artwork Placement

Here are a few useful tips about placement, size, and framing artwork:

- ▶ Explore canvas and floating frames versus framed art. Canvas is a less expensive option and will give you a more contemporary look. It is especially good for large pieces and your own photos. But for a more classy and expensive look, go with frames.
- ▶ Do not hang your art too high. It is best to hang it at the eye level of the average person's height.
- ▶ For above the sofa, allow about 10 inches between the top of the sofa and the bottom of the picture, or measure it when you sit on the sofa. You want to make sure when you or your family members sit on the sofa, you don't touch the picture behind you with your head. You will feel more relaxed this way.
- ▶ Above the sofa, one large or three smaller pictures look the most harmonious.
- ▶ When hanging three pictures, their length should not exceed the length of the sofa—approximately two-thirds of the total length of the sofa is ideal.
- ▶ Galleries are a great way to display family photos. Using a variety of sizes makes the composition more interesting than hanging them in straight rows.

We will touch more on art in Part III, when we work in different rooms of the house. Now it is time to get immersed in the abundant world of accessories.

CHAPTER 8

Building Block Six—
Accessories

 imilar to art, accessories are fun and easy to work with. It's a rich world of shapes, colors, and textures. It is great if the accessory means something to you or evokes an emotion.

Like art, accessories can trigger positive feelings such as pleasure, happiness, confidence, nourishment, abundance, and more. But they can trigger negative emotions and bring up difficult memories as well. If it is meaningless and neutral, then it will just be sitting there, hardly noticeable, taking precious space and collecting dust.

Like art, accessories can be used for balancing the Five Elements in the room and projecting a positive feeling. Below are examples of accessories categorized by the Five Elements.

Yin/Yang and the Five Elements in Accessories

Yin accessories: small-sized, refined, delicate, soft pieces; dark or neutral colored; organic or round shaped.

Yang accessories: large-sized, hard items; brightly colored or shiny; angular shaped.

Wood Element

The best way to bring Wood Element is using green color and live plants, as well as views of green trees through the windows, but any tall vertical object like ladders or long and thin objects are considered to be Wood Element as well.

Fire Element

Lamps, candles; bright red- or orange-colored items, such as sofa pillows or throw blankets, red pots and vases, red and orange flowers (live or artificial); exotic floral fabric patterns and leather materials. Pink- and purple-colored items are also in the category of Fire, but gentle or yin Fire. Fire Element is also expressed in triangular- or pyramid-shaped items.

Earth Element

Yellow or tan pillows and throw blankets; natural crystals and gemstones like white quartz, rose quartz, or citrine; objects made of clay, ceramic, and stone. Earth Element is represented by square-shaped objects.

Metal Element

Wall clocks, coins, bells, any objects made of metal, such as fireplace tools, wall art, vases, and wind chimes. Metal colors are gold, chrome, silver, or white. Metal shapes are round or oval.

Water Element

Fish tanks and water fountains are the strongest expression of Water Element accessories. Despite being high maintenance, fish tanks are an old-time favorite water feature and bring joy and good energy to a home. In classical feng shui, fish tanks are especially associated with prosperity, because there is always movement in the water with fish in it. Blue glass vases or glass statues of dolphins and fish, blue blankets, and rugs are another way to bring some vibrations of Water energy. Organic and wavy shapes also belong in the category of Water Element.

We will discuss the use of accessories in each room in Part III. There is an interesting category of accessories that are talismans and special objects that are worth talking about separately.

Special Nature Objects and Talismans

The use of talismans and special objects is ancient. A talisman can be natural or man-made, and, in most cases, is believed to be able to bring protection or good fortune. A talisman is an object with a concentrated energy that is supposed to influence the energy of the space and people in a positive way. Talismans can be cultural, religious, or personal. Placing a horseshoe above the door for good luck is an example of a cultural talisman. Placing an icon of Jesus or Mary above the front door is an example of a religious talisman in Christian culture. In Indian culture, a statue of Ganesha placed in the house is believed to clear obstacles and help to move forward in life. In Jewish culture, a Hamsa Hand is supposed to bring blessings and protection for the family.

A **special nature object** can be a rock or gemstone found or purchased in a place with special and beautiful natural energies. Either it will still have some of these energies in it, or it can help you remember and connect with a place you visited. This rock, seashell, or gemstone can become a personal talisman for you. They emanate energy of the sun, earth, water, and sky along with the relaxation and happiness you felt at that time. You felt something different than in everyday life, something more, perhaps a connection with your higher self or a life force of the particular place. Those rocks and shells help to connect you with that state of mind and a particular positive feeling or opening you had at that time. This is why we pick up those rocks and shells and bring them home. We may even feel that they have a healing effect on us. Certain natural quartz clusters or other gemstones have a refined, concentrated, harmonizing, and possibly, even healing energy.

I use gemstones differently from how people typically use them. I don't know too much about the meanings of crystals and all their nuances. I pick those with strong and pure vibrations of the natural energy of the earth and put them in one or two places in the house where Earth Element needs to be strengthened. I make sure it is aesthetically appropriate, and a gemstone will add something positive to the overall feeling of the room. Mostly, I use white quartz clusters and large pieces of rose quartz. If you put them in the right place, the area feels like an acupuncture point that emanates strong energy and strengthens the energy field of the room.

Another example of a talisman is a cherished piece of jewelry that you may have a special affinity with or bought during a time of transition in your life. It can be a gift from a special person or an item you bought in a special place. I bought such a piece on the last day of my engineering job. I went to the mall during my lunch break and saw this very unusual and rare blue opal in a white gold setting, so I bought it. I am not the jewelry type, and it was the first piece of expensive jewelry I have ever bought for myself. After I came back to work, my company announced a massive layoff due to the telecommunication industry collapse. I was happy because I knew that my new life phase had just begun. Shortly after the layoff, I made a decision to go to China and study feng shui there. So, the ring represents my new life and my new profession. My clients often comment on how beautiful my ring is and ask the name of the stone. I have never seen a stone like it again.

A **special object** can be an item that has been in a family for generations and cherished by that family. It may have meaning and an emotional connotation, and it can become a family talisman. Some may believe it brings positive energy and luck for the family. Some old family photos of your ancestors or something you inherited from your beloved grandmother or grandfather and want to pass along to your children might be such a talisman for your family. These items can be displayed alone if they are a large size. If they are smaller, you can put a few such items together and create an area of strong emotional response and meaning. These groupings are called altars.

Sometimes I intuitively feel a strong ancestral line in certain families. It feels like a certain similar quality that some family members share. I work with women more often than I work with men, and sometimes I feel a certain similarity between a mother and a daughter or more than one daughter. I remember a family with four daughters. All four of them and their mother had a certain similar feeling around them. The best way I can describe it was a feeling of feminine strength, grace, depth, and authentic spirituality that is not learned. I asked if the woman's mother or grandmother had something similar, and the answer was that both of them were strong, hardworking, respected, and spiritual in the ways that were available at the time. As we were talking about their female ancestral line, the presences of my client's mother, grandmother, and great grandmother were felt strongly by me and my client, almost like they were in the room with us. I asked my client to find a picture of them and create an ancestral altar in her home office. Along with photos of her ancestors she placed a photo of her four daughters and herself, a statue of the Divine Mother, some special gemstones, and a few other meaningful items. This helped her to feel stronger, more supported, and hold a sense of togetherness between her daughters while going through a tough divorce.

Altars

Altars are our way of letting the universe know what we want and our way of expressing gratitude to the spiritual divine energy for the blessings we receive.

You can create an altar for anything important in your life. There are two kinds of altars that we can work with that are relevant to the content of this book. The first one is more specific and used to express your wanting and aspirations for the next phase of your life. For example, you want to improve your existing relationships or, if you are single, you are ready for a new partner. Other examples are you want a new career path, you feel you might be due for a raise at your current job, or you need healing for your family and yourself. In this case, you put together a few items that represent this particular aspect you are working with.

If your aspiration is to improve your current relationship, you can place a photo of yourself and your partner that was taken when you were happy and two pieces of rose quartz with a small orchid or a beautiful soft lamp on a dresser in your bedroom.

An example of a prosperity altar could be a laughing Buddha statue, a jade plant, a string of coins, and an amethyst gemstone. It doesn't have to be a laughing Buddha, or anything described here. The most important thing is that these items resonate with you.

You can also write your goals and aspirations on a piece of paper and put it in a red envelope on your altar. Red has a strong vibration of action, so it will strengthen the energy of your aspiration.

The second kind of altar is a more general or gratitude-focused kind. It could be a spiritual altar depicting a deity that you are connected with such as the Buddha, the Archangel Michael, the Divine Mother, Quan Yin, or Ganesha. It could be a family or ancestor's altar.

The altar can be placed in the northwestern room or northwestern part of a room—the helpful people area—if the room function is appropriate for such a thing or if there is an appropriate place in the room for it. For most people, it might be a good idea to keep such an altar in a more private area, such as your home office, your bedroom, or on the bookshelf of your family room.

The altar will work better for you if you light a candle or burn incense sometimes. The act of lighting a candle or burning incense is an act of offering our gratitude to the divine beings and ancestors for their continuing blessings and support.

Family Photos

We all have so many gorgeous photos of our kids and family! They carry all the special moments of happiness, fulfillment, and pride for our families and our children's achievements. I see in many homes that it is difficult to say "enough" to the amount of photos on display. I am not immune to it either. Children growing up, happy family events, marriages, professionally done photos, or our own travel photos create a happy family story, and it definitely needs to be displayed and honored. But what happens is that some of us end up with photos on every single horizontal surface, and we can't even see what's in the third row anymore. A beautiful thing eventually becomes clutter.

The best way to display family photos is to create a family gallery on a wall. You can dedicate a family room wall to this, but from experience, the best place is usually a second floor landing wall or a hallway between bedrooms. It is great fun and becomes an art piece if you display those images using different sizes, different colors and styles of frames, or a frameless canvas style. It is a creative project that you may enjoy doing together with your kids.

No matter how beautiful and meaningful accessories and special objects are, a soulful home cannot be without real live plants. In the next chapter, let us dive into the world of house plants.

CHAPTER 9

Building Block Seven— Plants

House plants are incredible living things in so many ways! I am a big proponent of having real plants in the house.

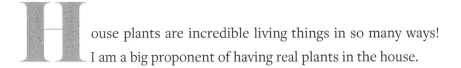

Not all plants are equal; some of them have better aesthetic qualities, while others would be more useful for cleansing the air from electromagnetic and environmental pollutants.

Plants can be happy and vibrant or stressed and depleted. If you choose to have living plants, you must take good care of them. You don't want suffering or dying energy in your home.

I have noticed that some people have a certain plant phobia. They claim that every plant they bring home dies. You might be surprised how easy it is to take care of a plant. If you treat it as not just a part of your décor, but something that is alive, you might remember that it needs nourishment from you once in a while. If you can take care of a child or a pet, then you can definitely take care of a plant.

There is a fascinating book by Peter Tompkins and Christopher Bird called *The Secret Life of Plants* that experimentally confirms that plants have emotions and feelings. They respond to our emotions and different kinds of thoughts we send toward them. I have lots of experience watching my husband growing plants from seeds that we bring from our tropical trips from around the world. He definitely gets a kick out of watching those little saplings coming out of the soil and getting stronger week by week, transforming into beautiful and sometimes unusual trees. I personally think he gives them love and care, and they respond to him, but he himself claims that all you need to do is give them water on a consistent schedule, once a week on a certain day.

Most plants would thrive near southeastern, southern, and southwestern windows with plenty of sun, but there are some that will do well by northern windows.

If you can't take care of plants, then your next best choice is art that has trees in it or silk plants. I prefer images of plants because it is rare that silk plants look natural and alive. Eventually they collect dust and start to feel tired. Silk flowers somehow look better than silk trees. Often silk flowers are indistinguishable from real flowers, while it is rare to find a silk tree that doesn't look fake, unless you pay a substantial amount of money for it.

Feng shui enthusiasts love plants with rounded leaves rather than long and spiky ones. They have a more harmonious feel to them. A jade plant with its rounded leaves that resemble coins and so-called "money plants" are loved by feng shui enthusiasts, but there are other amazing plants that will enhance the energy in your home in many different ways.

Yin/Yang and the Five Elements in Plants

All plants, especially the larger ones, are considered to be Wood Element. Flowering plants can add Fire Element in addition to the Wood, especially if flowers are red, purple, orange, or pink.

Large and tall plants such as the ficus tree, corn palm, and fiddle-leaf fig tree are yang Wood Element. Small and medium plants are yin Wood Element.

The areas that benefit from larger plants or trees are usually east, southeast, and south. It's best if you can place the plant close to the window so it gets plenty of light. In all other areas of the Bagua, I prefer to use smaller or medium-sized plants. Technically, Wood Element is not needed there, but we should not treat the house and the Bagua application mechanically. Plants are so much more than just Wood Element. They infuse the house with life force and joy and much more, which you will read about in the next section.

Multiple Uses and Benefits of Plants

▶ Plants bring vitality to our living and working spaces. They are living things, part of nature. Use them for increasing and uplifting energy in your space and beautifying your home. Place them in the areas of your home that you spend time in.

▶ Definitely have plants at your home office or at your workplace. Numerous studies were done over the last two decades on how plants boost energy, reduce stress, reduce eye fatigue caused by computer screens, and enhance mood and creativity. Plants increase productivity and happiness in offices. Dr. Chris Knight, a psychologist from Exeter University, conducted a ten-year study in which he found "the employees were 15 percent more productive when 'lean' workplaces are filled with just a few houseplants. When plants were brought into the offices—one plant per square meter—employee performance on memory retention and other basic tests improved substantially."

▸ Plants reduce stress. A study led by environmental psychology expert Dr. Tina Bringslimark at the Norwegian University found that the presence of house plants in offices reduces fatigue, stress, dry throat, and dry skin among office workers. Results showed that the more plants employees could see from their desks, the less sick-leave days they took! This study was repeated by several other experts with similar results.

▸ Plants remove toxins from the air and improve air quality. A NASA Clean Air Study suggests that plants naturally remove toxic agents from the air such as benzene, formaldehyde, trichloroethylene, ammonia, and others. You can find the list of plants that remove specific chemicals in the NASA Clean Air Study.

▸ NASA also found that plants absorb electromagnetic radiation and free radicals. These studies were done for the astronauts who work in a space station full of equipment, but are applicable to modern offices that are full of computers and wireless equipment. Many of us work from home, so our home offices often have quite a few pieces of equipment plus wireless internet. Although these experiments were performed in a sealed space station environment, and the results might not fully apply to typical buildings, you get the idea that there is much more to plants than the eye can see.

▶ According to the Bagua diagram, use plants for boosting the prosperity aspect in the southeastern area of your home, reputation aspect in the southern part, and health and growth in the east.

The plants that made the top of the list in various studies and also have good feng shui and aesthetic qualities are golden pothos, peace lily, snake plant, corn plant, rubber plant, English ivy, and Boston fern.

There are some other beautiful plants that didn't make the EMF and air pollution cleansing lists. I assume that not all the plants in the universe were tested, but some of them are beautiful and easy to care for. Among them are the Ficus tree, jade plant, ZZ plant (*Zamioculcas zamiifolia*), corn palm plant (*Dracaena fragrans*), bamboo stalk, and orchid flower.

Bamboo stalks are best placed in the east or southeast because bamboo grows fast and therefore has strong Wood Element quality, but they can be used anywhere you need a fast solution to uplift the energy. For example, if your bathroom is in the east (family and health), southeast (prosperity), or south (reputation), placing three stalks of healthy bamboo will help to uplift the energy there.

Orchids are especially gorgeous. They give so much joy because of their beauty and variety of colors and shapes. They are great anywhere in the house. Typically, they can shoot a new stem every six to eight months if you don't abandon them after they bloom and keep watering them regularly.

The ZZ plant can be used in darker areas such as western, northwestern, northern, or northeastern. According to the Bagua, we don't need a strong Wood Element in these directions, but it definitely will not hurt to have a few healthy but not too large plants there to bring vitality.

Now that you've learned about the building blocks of a soulful home, let's put it all together, one room at a time.

PART III

Putting It All Together

S ometimes what we see in a person's home can be totally unexpected. We can be pleasantly or unpleasantly surprised. Understandably, we often feel vulnerable inviting people to our home. It is so true what Oprah said: "When you invite people to your home, you invite them to yourself." What if people see something that we don't want them to see? What if they judge us? Let's reverse it. Let's design a home that we are proud to invite people into, a home that reflects our warmth, kindness, freedom, creativity, and the beauty of our soul. Most importantly, a home where we can be ourselves, feeling comfortable and relaxed, nourished and loved.

What makes a house feel special? What are the magical ingredients? The aim of this part of the book is to put all the foundations and building blocks we have discussed together and create each room as a soulful space. Pay special attention to the descriptions of the meaning of the rooms as they hold the keys to the soulful spaces beyond the functionality and material aspects. We'll begin with the entrance.

CHAPTER 10

Your Home's Entrance

When you approach someone's home, especially for the first time, all your senses become engaged. There is a certain excitement and a fascination with "what is this house about?" Even if you don't ask this question consciously, it is there in your subconscious mind. Humans are always intrigued by something new and unknown. We love new experiences and discovering new things. Visiting someone's home for the first time is similar to meeting a new person. The first impression, which is the feeling before your thinking mind kicks in, is usually right-on.

Often the entrance may express the essence of the home or give a little taste of what the household is about. It is a good idea to consciously create this feeling with color, art, and accessories.

In traditional feng shui there is a term, *Ming Tang*, which translates as a "bright hall." Ming Tang includes the entryway, the front door, porch, and the approach to the house. Ming Tang is a place where good energy is supposed to accumulate before entering a house and, upon entering it, ensures a proper distribution of this energy throughout the house. It is supposed to welcome you when you come home and create a positive first impression for whoever enters the house. This is a place where an important alchemical action happens.

> *All the good and plentiful energy that is part of the land, nature, and landscaping nourishes the house and is transformed into the energy of abundance, well-being, and harmony for the family. This is why we want the space in front of the house, the approach to the house, and the entryway to be the most welcoming and beautiful.*

It is a different feeling to enter into a well-lit, elegant, and sizable entrance compared with a small, cluttered, and dark one. We will discuss a few tricks in this chapter on how to make a small entrance feel larger by using art, mirrors, and colors.

Main Door

The main door is called the Mouth of Chi and has a large significance in traditional feng shui. When feng shui is used during the building stage of a new home or office, numerous principles and techniques including the Bagua and the Flying Star are used to place the main door in the position that will ensure that the energy surrounding the front door is beneficial for prosperity and good health. But it is not feasible for most people to build their house, nor is it practical to change the position of the front door.

Based on my experience and observations, the importance of the front door placement is overrated in modern times, with a large fraction of homeowners entering their homes through the garage. Larger homes typically have two entrances and therefore two front doors, the main door and the mudroom door. In most cases the mudroom door is the one used by family and guests because it is closer to the driveway or where people park.

I have observed that even if the placement of the door is not the best, according to the formulas and rules, there are a few things you can do to improve the energy:

- Make sure the door is not broken or stuck and opens and closes easily or as it should.
- Make sure your main door or mudroom door opens freely all the way; in other words, there is no stuff or furniture preventing it from fully opening. In both cases, it will make you feel irritated and stressed upon entering. This can be applied to any door in the house and especially the door being used the most.
- If you have two doors (a main door and mudroom door) and do not use the main door often, or if you enter from the garage most of the time, it would be great to open the main door once in a while, especially on a sunny day, to allow the energy to circulate and refresh. If you are not using the door at all, the energy becomes stagnant there, and this can weaken the energy in the area where you want it to be fresh and strong.
- Changing the color of the door helps to bring more auspiciousness and luck. Most importantly, if you love the color, it will help you feel happy and welcome every time you approach your house.

Main Door Color

Strengthening and inviting good energy is the main reason behind the red door concept in feng shui.

Red is energizing, catchy, and beautiful. But, not every door is created equal, and not every door has to be red. The main concept is that we want the door to be noticed. Whether it is red, blue, purple, or a stained wooden door, we want it to stand out. If you love the color and the design of the door, even if it is not totally feng shui compliant, you will feel mostly welcomed and happy upon entering or even just seeing the door.

You also have to make sure there is a balance between the color of the door and the home exterior color. Do not use a similar shade. You want to create a contrast, but the contrast has to be harmonious. Some colors just don't go together well, like a yellow house with an orange door or a pink house with a red door.

Red is an easy color for the door because red goes well with most exterior colors. Red goes especially well with gray, white, or other neutral light exteriors and brick walls.

A bright cobalt blue is another favorite color for the door. It goes well with light and neutral but warm exterior colors and looks especially beautiful with brick houses.

A green exterior would look great with a purple or deep pink door.

Orange or yellow doors may look pretty with a green exterior. Blue exteriors would look best with a maroon or yellow door. Yellow houses look very interesting with hot pink or purple doors.

Many people ask me whether the house will lose its auspiciousness if they use natural stained wood doors rather than painted doors. The answer is no, the house will not lose its auspiciousness. Most houses look great with a stained wood door, especially if it is a patterned stained door. If the stained wood door doesn't stand out, you may want to direct some attention to it by using wreaths, lights, and planters with flowers.

Stained wood doors often have some glass in them or side lights around them. Although these doors are quite beautiful at times, I suggest minimizing the amount of glass, or choose satin glass rather than clear glass. You will feel more private and secure this way.

White or gray doors are simply boring. There is not much energy in them, which is the opposite from our goal—to attract and invite energy. I am not a big fan of black doors either. Although it may look classy, the color black doesn't have much energy in it.

For the majority of houses that face south, southeast, or southwest direction, a red, pink, purple, or natural wood door is a good choice. For the north-facing house the best choice would be a rich cobalt blue. I would not recommend using a bright red in the north (Fire and Water clash), but, rather, more toned-down colors like purple. East and north-east doors would benefit from blue, turquoise, or green. West-facing houses benefit from yellow-colored doors; not-so-bright reds can be used here as well. For the northwest-facing houses, I recommend deep purple or blue doors.

Yin/Yang and the Five Elements in the Entrance

The entrance would most definitely benefit from more yang and less yin energy. This often is reflected by the architecture such as high ceilings or making an entrance open to the second floor (spacious and bright). This feels more welcoming than a yin entrance (small and dark).

There is no predominant Element that specifically has to be at the entrance. Every entrance is different and would benefit from different Elements.

Wood Element provides the feeling of spaciousness and vitality. The Wood is represented in high ceiling entrance designs or live plants or pictures of plants.

The feeling of warmth and welcoming is created by **Fire Element**. This could be represented in a chandelier, live flowers, and art with red, orange, pink, and purple colors.

Earth Element brings a feeling of a different kind of warmth and connection with nature. Examples are an earthy landscape of meadows and hills, a ceramic or clay vase, or a natural fiber entry rug.

The presence of **Metal Element** is best expressed by good organization, a convenient closet system, cleanness, and light, pastel colors.

Water Element in art or fountains brings an energizing or relaxing feeling.

Entrance Wall Color

Typically, I like to use a neutral color at the entrance—something that is light, warm, spacious, and uplifting. It's rare that I would advise using dark, bold, or very rich colors at the entrance, because they have a tendency to make the space look and feel smaller.

We often see a hallway and several other rooms from the entrance, and if they are painted in different colors, it is best to use a neutral and light color at the entrance so it doesn't interfere with and ties all the other colors together well. If there is a stairway at the entrance, it is best to use the same color for the entrance, stairway, and the second floor landing because it is all connected. Dark colors never work well for a stairway or hallway because typically they are long and narrow, and the dark color will make the space feel contracted and even claustrophobic. Even if the stairway is open to the second floor, it is a large area, and painting it a bold and dark color will take away from the feeling of spaciousness that we may want to create at the entrance.

If your entrance is a separate room, you don't see too many other rooms, and your foyer is not open to the second floor, then there is more room for play. You can use a bolder, brighter color, especially if there is a particular color that gives you joy. If your entrance doesn't have much natural light, then using light yellow or light green colors is quite appropriate. Blues are on the colder side are typically not used at the entrance much. In most cases, an off-white with hints of tan, gray, or cream would be your best choice.

On rare occasions for some homes, a more saturated color might be appropriate. For example, I've been working with a client on renovating an old Victorian home located on top of a hill, with a great view of Boston. The house has the look and feel of a castle. Rich, dark colors were used throughout the house to accentuate the unusual personality and beauty of the rooms. The grand foyer was located in the south. South relates to the fame and reputation aspect, and it was perfect to bring a variation of rich, red color. I was a bit nervous to use rich red on the walls, but my client wanted to give it a try. There was plenty of light coming through the large windows and together with brass lamps, dark furniture, and gold accents, it created a great atmosphere, and the essence of the house was expressed well.

Entrance Furniture and Energy Flow

If there is one area in the house where you cannot have clutter, it's the entrance. If it is cluttered, energy can't move freely and the entire house will be depleted. In addition, every time you enter the house, you will feel stressed. If you have a large family and no mudroom with designated closets and shelving, it is the hardest thing to maintain those shoes, coats, and backpacks at the entrance in a tidy way. If you are not satisfied with your closet system, I highly recommend spending some time and rethinking how the organization might be improved. Even if you need to build a larger closet space or add additional shelving in your existing closet, it will be worth the effort. Ikea and the Container Store have some good options. Sometimes, if space allows, I suggest using ottomans or benches (see Diagram 5) with storage for shoes or hats and gloves inside them. It's quite comfortable when we need to sit to put certain shoes or boots on. You have to make sure, however, that nothing prevents opening the door fully and nothing is blocking the entrance.

It is great to have an entryway console table on the side from the entry door. A table with small drawers will help to keep keys, sunglasses, and other small items hidden so they are not on the surface. A mirror above the table is a plus, but make sure the mirror is not placed across the entry door, but on a side (see Diagram 5).

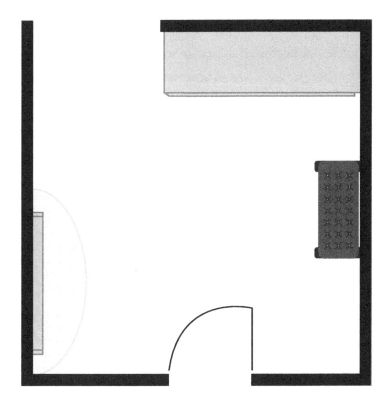

Diagram 5: Entrance

If the entryway is large enough, a round table in the middle can be used. It is a harmonious way to slow the energy down and experience a beautiful room.

Tables with rounded corners or half-moon tables often work well for small entrances, especially if the configuration of your entryway is such that a rectangular table's corner would be aimed at you upon entering. If your entryway is very small, do not place any furniture in it but place a piece of art with an ocean or meadow to create the illusion of a bigger space. We will discuss this more in the Art section.

I remember a client who told me that she was not comfortable entering her house. She perceived a threat of some kind every time she entered it. She even thought there was an unfriendly spirit living there. She didn't have a separate entry room but entered through her living room, and there was an open bookshelf with particularly sharp features only one or two feet away from the entry door. Every time she entered the house, she would get "hit" by the sharp lines and corners of the book shelf's edges. In addition, there was a large, bulky chair only four feet away from the door, pushing energy away and creating a blockage. This was definitely not a welcoming situation. My client was a sensitive person, and, not surprisingly, her mind translated those interior aspects as threatening. We moved things around, freeing the entrance from the shelf and the chair, and my client's feeling upon entering her house completely changed. This kind of scenario can happen in any entryway. Make sure that nothing points at you when you open the door, whether it is a sharp corner of the entryway table or even a plant with pointy leaves.

Mirrors are quite beneficial at the entrance. They visually increase the space and if placed so they reflect either nature in the window across or a beautiful piece of art, they will multiply all the positivity and beauty. Always make sure that mirrors reflect something you want to see plenty of. Pay attention that a mirror doesn't reflect sharp corners of the furniture or sharp architectural details. Do not place a mirror in front of the main entry door. First, it would be weird to see yourself right after you open the door; and second, it would reflect all the beneficial energy you want to invite in right back.

An entrance rug or a mat is usually a good idea. Besides collecting wetness or dirt from the outside, it brings a welcoming and softening feeling. A mat helps to create a separation of the outside and the inside. I like warm-colored rugs or mats in the entrance, and sometimes it is fun to use a bolder color here, especially if your entrance would benefit from a certain Element. A round shape is appropriate for larger, open entrances, especially if from the front door you can see the back door or a large window at the back of the house. A round rug helps to slow down the energy so it can be distributed throughout the house rather than leaving too fast.

Entrance Lighting

Lighting should be bright at the entrance. Ming Tang is a "bright hall," after all. Chandeliers should be proportional to the height and width of the entryway. A two-story open foyer requires a grand chandelier, crystal or a more contemporary style, like cascaded raindrop glass bubbles if you prefer, to fill the space proportionally to the height and size of the stairway. A ceiling pendant, crystal or glass, works well with a lower ceiling. Make sure a chandelier doesn't have too many sharp details. Rounded and smooth shapes are preferable. Also make sure that the chandelier or pendant produces enough light; you must pay attention to the wattage the appliance produces. Having it on a dimmer is convenient so you can adjust the amount of light according to your needs.

Entrance Art

Since the entrance is a formal area, I recommend using somewhat formal art and richer-looking frames here. Pick a piece with a positive, uplifting, and welcoming feeling, as it will be one of the first things you and your guests see upon entering the house. Colorful landscapes, especially if they are meaningful to you, or pictures of flowers that you love work well at the entrance. Water art might work well in the entryway, too, because water is associated with prosperity and wealth and brings the quality of expansiveness and relaxation. If the picture is too neutral to you or the colors are boring, you will not get a welcome feeling upon entering.

Even a small entryway can become welcoming and spacious if you add a picture of nature with warm colors that also features open spaces, such as an ocean, lake, or meadow. The effect will be even stronger if you place a mirror across from it to reflect the picture.

Entrance Accessories and Talismans

Since the entrance space is usually limited, it is not a great place for accessories, but if the space allows for a special item to be displayed, then do it. A beautiful lamp would work well on the entryway console table to be used at times when you prefer less wattage to the ambient lighting of a chandelier.

Entrance Plants

Not too many entrances have enough space for larger plants, but if you can fit a small or medium green leafy plant on the floor or on a short stand (making sure that they don't obstruct the energy flow), you will be pleased with the results. It is easy and a good practice to regularly place cut flowers or an orchid on the entryway table. It brings joy.

Special Cases

In many older two-story houses, the stairway is often close to the front door. It may create a cramped feeling upon entering, and your eyes will be drawn upstairs, which is not necessarily the effect you want to have right after you enter the house. Similarly with split-level homes, the split is often too close to the entry door and your eyes will be drawn downstairs. In cases like these, hanging a bright piece of art in the entryway will help to distract the attention and direct energy and people to where you want them to go after they enter the house.

If you don't have an entryway and enter the house straight into the family or living room, it's great to create some separation from the rest of the room rather than entering straight into a large room. At a minimum, you can place an entryway rug to create some separation. You can also experiment with a privacy screen or room divider either on the side of the door or across from the door. I rarely like the use of Japanese rice paper screens—they often feel like they do not belong to the space or are too flimsy for the entrance anyway. Look for a carved wooden screen. It can be a beautiful feature if the screen is partially see-through. Sometimes it is worth it to build a half wall on the side like in Diagram 6. It creates enough separation from the family room so people sitting on the sofa or in a chair don't feel too exposed.

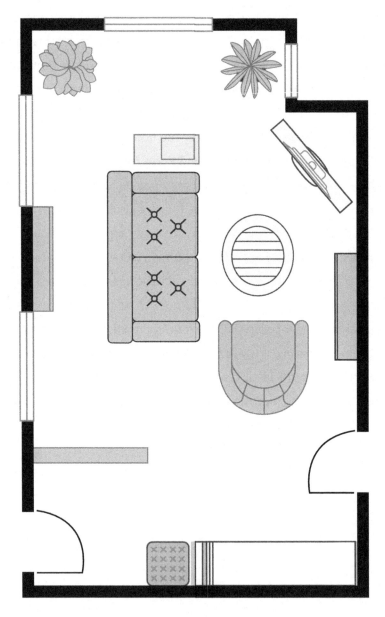

Diagram 6: Separating the entrance from the family room

The next room we naturally transition to is the kitchen. People who deal with real estate know that the kitchen is the room that attracts most buyers. If it is large and well-designed or newly remodeled, the house will sell faster.

CHAPTER 11

The Kitchen

The kitchen is the heart of the home. One can certainly say it is the belly of the home too! It is the most active and most used area in many houses. It is an alchemical and creative place where food items are transformed into nourishment for the body.

It is also a place where communication between family members happens quite often. People do not use dining rooms anymore for everyday eating and, in most houses, the eating area is right next to the kitchen, which makes the kitchen a central gathering place and a communication hub for a family. When we have parties, no matter how much we try to confine people to a family room or a living room, people are attracted to kitchens like moths are attracted to light. Perhaps it's because kitchens inherently have warm and nourishing energy. To support all these activities, we need to have a good quality, amount, and flow of energy in the kitchen.

Yin/Yang, the Five Elements, and Energy Flow in the Kitchen

The kitchen is a place of many activities; therefore, its design should be oriented more toward yang rather than yin features and elements. This is typically achieved with natural light during the daylight hours and sufficient lighting in the evenings, lighter wood or white cabinets, and adding a few bright colors in art and accessories.

There is something special about starting our day in a sunlit kitchen. Having the kitchen in the east or southeast of the home is a favorite kitchen placement in feng shui architectural design, which can be traced back hundreds of years. Modern science confirms that being exposed to sunlight in the morning regulates our circadian rhythms and increases serotonin hormone production, which makes us happier and more resilient to stress. If your kitchen is in the northern part of the house where there is no direct sunlight, pay attention to the section on colors. Introducing a color that brings the qualities of warmth and sunshine will be helpful.

Fire Element is considered to be an important Element in the kitchen. Although we may not cook with open fire the way we did in ancient times, people who love cooking and cook a lot prefer gas to electric stoves. They claim (and I am with them too) it works better, but I also think there is something so natural and satisfying for us to see and use the actual flame. In traditional feng shui, Fire Element in the kitchen relates to wealth. We want to pay attention to the location of the stove.

There are three main appliances in the kitchen: stove, sink, and fridge and, therefore, three different types of energy: Fire (the stove), Water (the sink), and Metal (the fridge). These three Elements interact with each other. Water puts Fire out, and Metal cools Fire down. Also, the stove is the most yang object in the kitchen and the fridge is the most yin. Practically speaking, keeping the hottest and the coldest appliance next to each other doesn't feel right. It's best if these three objects with very different energies are separated. This is why a triangular design for the kitchen is best. The three diagrams below describe three different kitchens' configurations, but all of them embrace this principle of separation of the three main appliances. This design doesn't need to have any esoteric basis; in fact, it is a preferred design by most architects as it is the most convenient for traffic, energy flow, and food preparation. If you cook a lot, you know well that it is great to have free working areas between the stove and sink.

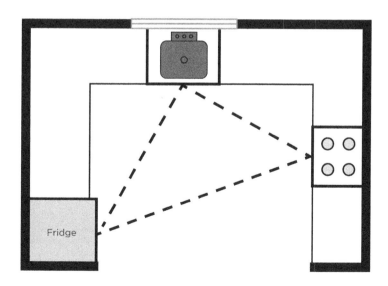

Diagram 7: Triangular design in the bracket-shaped kitchen

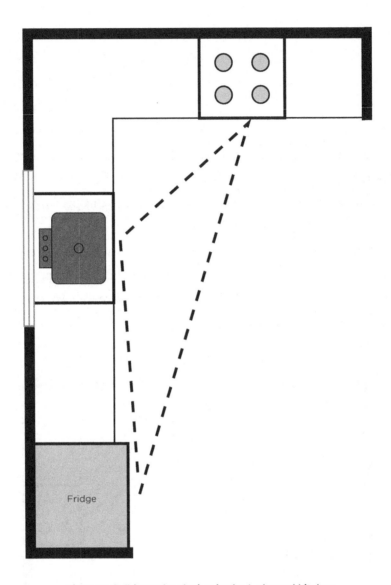

Diagram 8: Triangular design in the L-shaped kitchen

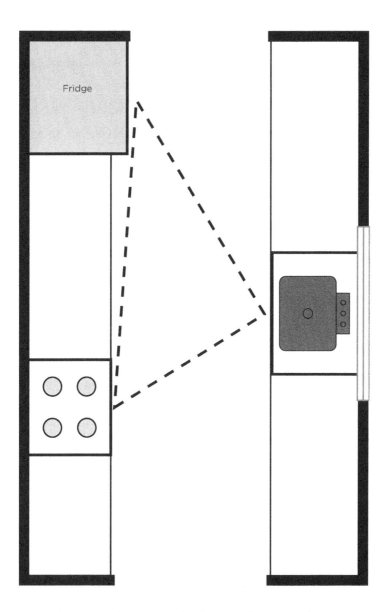

Diagram 9: Triangular design in the train-shaped kitchen

If your stove is too close to the sink or the fridge, it would be a good idea to strengthen Fire Element around the stove. In the Art and Accessories sections, I will show you how to do it.

Earth Element is essential to the kitchen as well. Both Fire and Earth Elements are in harmony with each other and together they create a warm, energizing, and nourishing environment. Earth Element relates to nourishment and digestion. Also yellow, orange, and red are colors of the many fruits and vegetables, and they are appetizing colors! Fire and Earth are natural Elements to the kitchen environment. This is the main reason to strengthen these two Elements in the kitchen.

Some amount of Wood Element is good in the kitchen as well. Wood nourishes the Fire and adds to the feeling of vitality. A few pots with herbs and other plants are welcome in the kitchen. Natural wood in cabinets and floors brings warmth, beauty, and connection to nature.

Modern kitchens have a tendency these days to be mostly white with various stainless steel appliances. While white feels clean and bright, if there is too much of it, it creates a cold and unemotional environment. It's really good to bring colors and elements of Earth, Fire, and Wood into these environments to bring natural elements and create a feeling of comfort and joy.

There was a short period twenty years ago when stainless steel countertops were popular. It was called industrial kitchen design. My feng shui teacher Roger Green once told a story about a family in Italy. The story goes that the husband made a lot of money and decided to move his family from a smaller old home into a big contemporary house. He hired an expensive designer who implemented the latest trends in their new home. Within six months of moving, the forty-plus-year-old mother of the family got sick, and nobody could diagnose her. She became depressed, lost her appetite, and was staying in her room most of the day. Since doctors could not help, her husband hired a feng shui professional because she felt that the new house had something to do with her health decline.

My teacher was in Italy at that time, and he consulted for this family. He assessed the new home's energy, as well as the woman's energy, and he asked lots of questions about their old home. Even talking about their old home, she became more animated. This new home was definitely lacking the brighter colors and the natural Earth and Fire Elements that the woman was so used to.

Because she cooked a lot, her old kitchen environment was part of her energy. My teacher asked them to paint their white kitchen in rich yellow, get rid of the stainless steel countertop, and install natural earthy granite. He also suggested bringing in the usual Italian décor of fresh herbs, flowers in ceramic pots, and other traditional colorful objects. In a few months, the woman's health was restored, and her happiness came back. As I reflect back on this story, in addition to the right Elements, the old home had a soul, and the new one didn't. With the right colors and accessories, the new home began to transform into a home with a soul.

Other than the appliances, there is no need to implement additional Metal Element, and the kitchen is not the right place for Water Element.

It is great if the kitchen is spacious and energy can flow through it freely. If the kitchen is crowded with cabinets and furniture that is too large or placed too tightly, if there is clutter or just too many things on the countertops and inside the cabinets, the energy will have a tendency to get stuck and become the opposite of nourishing; it will be draining. If you need to, please review decluttering in Chapter 3. There are a few tips there on kitchen decluttering.

Kitchen Wall Colors

The color that carries the qualities that are essential in the kitchen and will support nourishing and communication functions is yellow. I like light shades that resemble sunshine and are not too saturated. Yellow goes very well with white or off white cabinets and most natural wood cabinets including dark wood. The shade of yellow has to be very carefully selected so there is a harmonious relationship between the color of the cabinets, countertop, and walls.

It is especially nurturing to add these sunny vibrations if your kitchen is in the darker and colder parts of the house such as west, northwest, north, and northeast sections. Earthy qualities of yellow are in harmony with west, northwest, and northeast directions. In the north, Earth Element is not so appropriate, but very light yellow or cream colors are Metal Element and, in the northern kitchens, will bring more brightness and warmth—just what is needed there.

If your kitchen is located in the southern part of the house, where there is plenty of light, you can use light sage green instead if the color speaks to you. The color green goes well in the south, southeast, and east kitchens because Wood is the native element of east and southeast, and Wood feeds the Fire of the south.

Although there is plenty of light in the afternoon, southwestern kitchens do well with a yellow color. Southwest relates to relationships and a woman's health. Introducing Earth Element and yellow color in the southwest kitchen strengthens these aspects. We can especially appreciate it in the darker and colder months of the year.

Although blue or aqua is used sometimes in kitchens, these colors do not belong here. They are of Water Element, and they are colder than the atmosphere in the kitchen should be. Avoid black appliances if you can because black relates to Water Element as well, and it is cold. If you think about it, blue is not an appetizing color. There is not much food associated with blue. This is another reason to avoid blue in the kitchen.

Gray or white kitchen walls are cold, unemotional, and don't help to create an atmosphere of a soulful kitchen that we tried to portray here. If your kitchen has too much white or gray and you don't want to repaint, then use red and yellow colors in accessories and art to balance it.

Kitchen Furniture

Kitchen cabinets, buffets, and stools around the island are in the category of kitchen furniture. From personal experience I can say that having cabinets that you don't like will irritate you every day, several times a day. Even if you are not consciously irritated, subconsciously you will feel dissatisfied. I've lived with cabinets that I very much disliked for several years, and every day I felt somewhat displeased when I was in the kitchen. The cabinets were new, so it was hard to justify changing them. When I finally changed them to something I adored, my mood in the kitchen improved dramatically, and it resulted in more happiness, better meals, and more harmony in my family.

If I had known how big a difference it would make, I would have done it sooner! If your kitchen is due for remodeling, do not delay, and make sure to choose the cabinets and the countertop that you will love. When you get a feeling of joy and satisfaction looking at them and using them every day, paying a little extra for what you really like will be well worth it.

I see how much joy people get from granite or quartz countertops. Granite can be like a piece of art that nature produced. It is very much worth it to spend the time and choose the right one for you.

If you have an island in your kitchen, stools are another way to bring color and style along with functionality.

Kitchen Lighting

Because the kitchen is a gathering place and a workplace, it needs plenty of ambient lighting and multiple task lighting areas. The best kitchens are the ones with windows and sliding doors to provide an abundance of natural lighting. Sinks are typically placed by the window to maximize natural lighting where it is needed the most. Recessed lighting cans or pendants should be strategically placed above the sink and areas where we cut and prepare food.

For a more uniform source of lighting in modern homes, cove or valance lighting is sometimes used. The stove needs to have its own task lighting. Under cabinet lighting is an awesome invention. I remember how much of a difference it made when I installed it in my kitchen after I remodeled it. Accent lighting inside glass-door cabinets can bring additional warmth and beauty to the kitchen. Placing a few red glasses in those cabinets will create a dramatic effect when the lights are on.

Kitchen Art

Art with red, orange, yellow, and green colors will look and feel great here. Bright colors will uplift your mood. It is a known fact that when we make food in a happy state of mind, the food will taste better. I had a client who moved into a brand-new home with slightly gray kitchen walls and white kitchen cabinets. It was a beautiful kitchen but felt sterile and needed life. She bought a large and gorgeous photo of tomatoes and placed it near the stove. Not only does it look awesome, but she claims it makes her happy when she is in the kitchen.

Kitchen Accessories

Adding a few red accessories in the kitchen not only strengthens Fire Element but brings joy. The esoteric side of having reds in the kitchen is that Fire energy works on strengthening the money aspect. It's very easy to test! Red kettle, red pots, a red utensil holder, a red floor mat, a red toaster, or any red KitchenAid appliance are some examples and easy ways to do it. You don't need to overdo it and add all of it—two or three items is best. Balance and aesthetics are important.

Cookbook covers, interesting dishes, and cups that are colorful work together to create a feeling of a soulful and happy place. I absolutely love having fresh fruits, vegetables, and herbs in the kitchen. Things like a woven fruit basket or ceramic vase bring the element of nature to the kitchen. This affinity with elements of nature is rooted far back in time for all of us. It is in our genes.

Natural elements, the gifts of Mother Earth, resonate stronger with us than man-made, all-white, metal, and glass spaces. I am not against contemporary spaces at all—I love most of them and have helped to create lots of them—but for us humans to thrive, we need to balance them with natural elements. When our spaces are balanced, we feel connected and grounded and happier as a result.

Kitchen Plants

The kitchen is not typically a room where we place plants, but it will make a big difference in your kitchen if you can do it. Plants bring life, beauty, and nature to spaces. They will also cleanse the air (see Chapter 9 on plants). A smaller plant, herbs, or cut flowers on a countertop are always great, but if the space allows, place a larger plant. Often people can place a few plants in so-called breakfast areas near the kitchen table.

Special Cases

Traditional feng shui states that if there is a bathroom behind the wall that hosts the stove, especially if there is a toilet, sink, shower, or any water pipes that run behind the stove, it will drain the Fire energy and therefore weaken wealth. I cannot attest to this statement completely and will not claim that this situation will drain your wealth, but intuitively I know it doesn't feel right to have a toilet behind the stove. Whether it relates to wealth or not, if the energy is compromised, it will do good to correct it.

I have had many clients comment that after they added some red items to the kitchen, something positive happened with the wealth aspect, but the truth is they had done several other prosperity-enhancing things in other areas of the home, so it is hard to separate. If in doubt, I would recommend strengthening Fire Element in the kitchen anyway. At a minimum, I can promise it will bring joy and fun to the kitchen.

You can also introduce a strong Wood Element to the bathroom that is adjacent to the stove wall. The Wood will uplift the energy that is going down the septic pipes. Adding bamboo or another vertical plant or picture of a plant above the toilet will also help.

I'd like to add a short digression here about the stove. We want the energy to collect rather than disperse around the stove. For this reason, we don't want the stove to be visible from the entrance. Admit it: it doesn't feel right to see the stove upon entering the house. If this is the case with your home, place a screen in the way if at all possible and aesthetically acceptable.

It is best if there is a solid wall behind the stove for a similar reason (so the energy is not dispersed at the stove location, but gathered). Yes, that is right, a solid wall behind the stove, rather than an island, is preferable. People who cook a lot prefer a solid wall behind the stove for practical reasons as well.

It is much easier to implement feng shui principles for the kitchen and the best stove placement when we build a new home or remodel the kitchen. Still, these tips will help a great deal to balance and enhance the energy.

The natural flow will take us from the kitchen to the dining room or eating area.

CHAPTER 12

The Dining Room

Many traditional homes have two eating areas, a formal dining room and the everyday eating area that is part of the kitchen or right next to the kitchen. Some contemporary homes with an open floor concept and newer apartments have only one eating area. On an everyday basis, most people eat in the area that is located in or close to the kitchen.

Having a separate room where we dine only on special occasions and holidays in traditional feng shui and in most cultures is associated with being wealthy.

Eating in a dining room allows one to create a ritual and tra-dition. This is a room where we share food prepared with love and care and good, meaningful conversation. This is a room where people share traditions and create strong connections between family members, extended family, and friends. When we decorate the dining room, we want to make sure that the room supports these wonderful aspects.

It is a little sad to see that in many houses dining rooms are being used only a few times a year during holidays. I am not saying that you should change your habits and use the dining room more often. It makes sense for a small family of two to four people to eat at a smaller table in the area that is close to the kitchen, but I will mention one negative aspect of using a dining room only a few times a year. The energy starts to stagnate there, especially if the dining room table accumulates papers, children's projects, or mail on it. It's very hard to resist placing things on a large horizontal surface if we don't have a good organizational system and designated spaces for storage. It's totally fine to use the dining room table for projects, but when things accumulate there it creates stagnation and stress.

Traditionally the dining room supports aspects of reputation and prosperity. I would like to add functions of nourishment and communication. The nature of these aspects and activities altogether is yang rather than yin; therefore, similar to the kitchen, we want the proportion of yin and yang energy to be shifted more toward yang in a room décor.

Yin/Yang and the Five Elements in the Dining Room and Eating Area

Since the dining room is a place where we socialize, it is best if it is more yang than yin. The yin room can be too relaxing or too cold for eating and socializing.

Examples of yang objects are light, wood furniture; crystal or other chandeliers; warm wall colors; red, orange, yellow, green, and purple colors in art and accessories; emotionally uplifting art; larger plants.

Examples of yin objects are any antique pieces of furniture, accessories, or art; dark wood in table chairs or buffet; blue, gray, beige, brown, black, and generally dark colors in art, rugs, and accessories.

Fire and Earth Elements should be present in the décor. Fire will support the reputation aspect, uplift the energy, and bring joy. Earth will support digestion and stimulate conversation. Metal Element is great here as well, but not in the form of white or gray walls. Gold or silver is associated with prosperity, therefore gold and silver in accessories will accentuate this aspect. Wood Element is often present in the dining room. A good quality buffet, table, and chairs are typically made of real wood. As I mentioned earlier, seeing the natural grain of the wood makes us relaxed and happy. Water Element is optional, depending on the Bagua sector. If your dining room is in the east, adding Water Element will support family harmony. If your dining room is in the southeast, Water will enhance prosperity. More importantly, the décor should make sense to you and reflect how you want to feel in the space.

If you don't have a formal dining room, some of these suggestions are applicable to your eating area. We want that area to have warm and nurturing qualities as well.

Examples of the Five Elements in the Dining Room

Wood

Green colors; plants, especially larger ones; pictures of trees; furniture made of lightly finished wood like maple, cherry, or walnut

Fire

Red, orange, or rich purple colors in an accent wall, art or chair upholstery; candles; chandeliers and other lighting

Earth

Rich yellow or terra-cotta colors; art that depicts earthy landscapes and abundance of nature; things made of earth like ceramic or clay vases and dishes

Metal

Clock; candleholders; chalices; metal frames; metal wall artwork

Water

Seascapes; pictures of boats; aquariums; water fountains; wavy organic shapes in curtains or rugs

Dining Room Colors

The most appropriate colors for the dining room walls are gold, yellow, orange, or coral. These saturated and rich colors will create the right atmosphere for the activities described earlier. It is a great room to use textured and more festive wallpaper if you prefer.

If your dining room is in the west or northwest section of the Bagua, using earthy or golden colors will support children and helpful people sectors of the Bagua. If it is in the north, a lighter yellow would be a good choice. For the southwest room, richer yellow, orange, coral, or pink are good color choices. For the south room, green, red or purple colors are appropriate. For the southeast, purple, green, or gold are best. And for the east and northeast, green or lighter yellow are good choices. Often painting an accent wall using a saturated color will create a more dramatic effect and be more interesting than painting the entire room.

The most unacceptable color for the dining room is blue. Blue is Water Element, and it is on the colder side of the color spectrum; therefore, it is too yin for the dining room. White or gray are not the most appropriate colors for the dining room either. They are also too cold, unemotional, and do not support socializing and dining activities. If you don't like to use bold colors, then using a warm neutral color is your best choice, but add a large piece of art with orange, red, purple, and yellow colors in it.

Dining Room Furniture and Energy Flow

We love soft edges and curves in feng shui. An oval shaped table or a round table are the most harmonious choices, but you will not find too many contemporary tables that are oval. Bow-shaped or rectangular tables are fine, but choose those with softened corners. A natural wood table is better than a painted table. Avoid glass and metal tables. Glass tables are cold, hard, and do not hold the energy. We want the table to be solid and hold everything on it in a graceful and nourishing way.

Either cushioned or not, chairs should be comfortable so you can enjoy several hours sitting in them at holiday dinners.

An area rug can add color and beauty to every dining room. There is also a functional side of using a rug. It will create a separate area and hold the energy of the table and chairs together, signifying the dining experience.

The dining room is a great place to have a mirror. Often it is placed above the serving buffet like in Diagram 10, but there are few things you should know about mirror placement. You want the mirror to reflect something nice like nature or a piece of art or some nice accessory. Here it is placed to reflect nature from the windows. If the mirror reflects stairs, banisters, sharp edges of furniture, a telephone pole, or a dead tree outside, then I would advise against placing a mirror in such a spot. You would be better off with a piece of artwork instead.

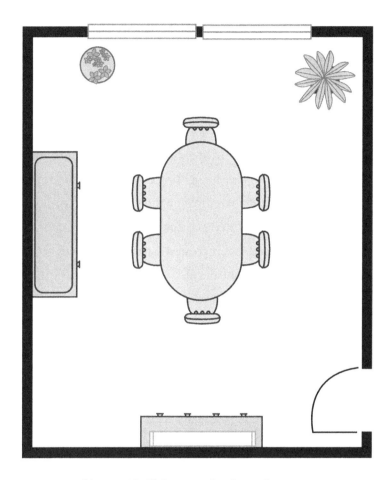

Diagram 10: Dining room furniture placement

A good energy flow is created in the dining room if it is spacious, doesn't have too many furniture pieces, and the table and chairs are not oversized or undersized. Fewer sharp corners and more softened edges will bring a sense of harmony and peace that your family and guests will enjoy and appreciate without even knowing why.

Dining Room Lighting

Chandeliers create ambient lighting around the table but also create a warm atmosphere and signify a sense of energy gathering around the table. It is a good idea to have your chandelier on a dimmer so you can change the mood by adjusting the level of light. Crystal and glass chandeliers are beautiful and festive, but be aware of the shadows some of them may create. It is best if you can see the lighting effects in person in the store.

Once I found the most incredible chandelier online for my client's dining room. It was a gold-tinted glass bubble chandelier, and when she installed it, we both agreed that it created too many shadows on the table. Because it was so beautiful, she decided to keep it, but we both saw that it would be better to have less shadows.

Fabric shade chandeliers have a softer, feminine, and more intimate feel to them. Chandeliers with a lot of metal in them feel more masculine and colder. Choose the one that helps you express the type of atmosphere you want to create in your dining room. Whichever option you are attracted to, avoid chandeliers with features that are too sharp as it will create unnecessary irritation.

Dining Room Art

Landscapes with a strong Earth Element in them like meadows and rolling hills or vineyards would make any dining room look and feel good. Images of Tuscany's hills and vineyards or Southern France's lavender fields are good examples.

Pictures of flowers and fruits are appropriate for dining rooms. They are easy to find and go well with the dining room atmosphere. Cherry or other blossoms are uplifting and beautiful to use in a dining room.

Waterscapes with sailboats traditionally represent wealth. Ancestral portraits or art made by ancestors represent fame and reputation are great for displaying in the dining room.

Dining Room Accessories and Special Items

Humans dined by candlelight much longer than we have with electricity. It's in our genes to enjoy firelight. Don't just have candle holders and candles for decoration, but use them when you especially want to have an intimate atmosphere. This is why it is good to have your chandelier on a dimmer. Display some beautiful silver or ceramic vases or plates. Perhaps you got some from your grandparents, or you acquired some special items yourself?

When the time comes to pass them on to your children or grandchildren, you may start a new family tradition that your descendants will be participating in and talking to their children about. Especially if there is an interesting story that comes with the item. Most importantly, though, it is your warmth, kindness, and care that will pass along with the items and create a legacy for your family.

I don't recommend water fountains or fish tanks in the dining room that much, because of the maintenance. I think beautiful images can do more for us than undermaintained indoor water fountains or fish tanks, but if you are sure you will be able to keep up with regular maintenance, then it is a great enhancement to your dining room.

Dining Room Plants

It's not the first time you've heard from me that plants bring vitality, beauty, and softness into any space. The dining room is an excellent place to have a larger plant. Since most plants like natural light, the corner between windows is a good place for a tree. A smaller plant can be placed on a plant stand in front of a window. A flowering plant will please your senses and enliven any dining room.

The next stop on our journey through the home will take us to the family room.

CHAPTER 13

The Family Room

The family room serves as an everyday gathering place for the entire family and for occasional use by the extended family and close friends. Sometimes the terms "family room" and "living room" are interchangeable and mean the same thing. However, larger homes have both a family room and a living room. In this case, the living room (sometimes also called a den) is reserved for occasional use, but mostly to exhibit some special furniture, art, and accessories.

The room I will refer to as the "family room" is the one that is used by the family on an everyday basis. This is a place where family members gather to engage in some activities or easy-flowing conversation.

> *These days, we have increasingly less time to just sit down as a family and talk, unless we are watching TV or eating, but we often even do those things at different times and in different rooms. If you want to change this dynamic and gather as a family, creating a warm, inviting, and engaging space with comfortable seating, where everyone feels supported and nourished, is the key.*

Since the family room hosts people with different personalities and different needs, it needs to be the most balanced room in the entire house. This can be achieved by balancing yin and yang energies and the Five Elements in the room.

Examples of Yin and Yang Objects in the Family Room

If there was a way of measuring the balance, it would be best to have a similar amount of yin and yang objects in the family room, which would create a sense of balance and stability.

Examples of yin objects are low furniture like coffee tables, chairs, or sofas; soft rugs or throw blankets; dark green, blue, gray, or beige colors; round or oval shapes.

Examples of yang objects are tall furniture like bookshelves; chandeliers and lamps; hardwood flooring; red, orange, yellow, bright green, or white colors; square, rectangular, and triangular shapes.

The presence of these opposite energies will help to create a sense of stability and balance. Balancing yin and yang means we need a similar amount of yin and yang objects and colors in the room. For example, low sofas, chairs, and coffee tables are balanced with bookshelves and pictures on the walls. A hardwood floor and wooden coffee table are balanced with soft rugs, sofa pillows, and throw blankets. Dark-colored sofas and floors can be balanced with bright pillows and bright art.

Examples of the Five Elements in the Family Room

Different people have different energy needs. While the energy of Fire is good for some, others thrive on the energy of Water, Wood, Earth, or Metal. Full expression of all Five Elements in the room brings harmony to the room itself and all the occupants of the home.

Wood

Plants, especially tall ones; pictures of trees; green color; tall lamp; book-shelves, especially if made of real wood and unpainted wood with a light finish

Fire

Fireplace; candles; chandeliers and lamps; exciting, dynamic art that depicts running horses, exotic animals, plants, and birds; floral fabric patterns; leather; pillows or accessories with red, orange, purple, and pink colors in them

Earth

Sofas, chairs, ottomans, square coffee tables (not glass); yellow, mus-tard, terra-cotta, or brown colors; pictures of mountains, meadows, or vineyards; ceramic or clay accessories; rocks or geodes; soft throw blankets, especially if earthy colors or a plaid pattern

Metal

Metal fireplace tools; clocks; white or gray color; round shapes; metal wall hangings; any accessories that incorporate metal, silver, gold, or chrome

Water

Aquariums, fountains, or pictures with water, boats, or fish; organic wavy patterns; blue colors; rugs, especially those with a less geometrical and more wavy, organic pattern; blue glass vases or blue pebbles

If you have items from all Five Elements present in your family room, then likely your space will have a sense of harmony, contentment, and completeness, and most people will feel very comfortable in it.

Family Room Colors

The most balanced color is green. It is not a coincidence that green is in the middle of the visible color spectrum chart. We evolved outside in nature, so green has a calming and comforting effect on our psyche. In many cases, I like using soft, muted, light, and warm greens on the family room walls. I choose shades that bring a calm yet joyful feeling and sense of vitality, expansion, and harmony. They are neutral enough to be used alongside many other colors.

If the room is dark in the northern part of the house, I like lighter and creamier greens on the walls. If the room has big windows, plenty of natural light, and is in the southern part of the house, I would use a cooler green with more grounding gray in it.

Sometimes people prefer a bolder choice of green, and some houses "accept it." This is the term I use if the color is in harmony with the house and the family. Some houses, just like people, are a little bit more shy, gentle, and subtle, and using bolder, brighter wall colors does not feel right. It feels forced and disharmonious, while other houses look and feel great with brighter colors.

Of course, neutral gray or tan is always a safe option too if you don't want to experiment. Make sure to choose a warm shade, though, otherwise people will not want to spend too much time in the family room.

In some very contemporary homes people choose a pure white color for their family room to accentuate architectural details. It is quite beautiful at times but not grounded enough and somewhat harsh, which makes the room not restful enough. Use the above guidelines to balance it.

Family Room Furniture and Energy Flow

All the furniture placement described in this section is aimed at creating a good flow that will support a sense of harmony, relaxation, and comfortable socializing in the family room.

There are often two main objects in the family room: the fireplace and TV, around which the sitting area is typically created. In interior design these objects are called focal points. Sometimes, sitting areas are created around focal points like a beautiful view of the ocean or lake or a distant mountain or even a special piece of art. Most families arrange their furniture around the TV, the fireplace, or both. If you have only one focal point, it is easy to create a sitting area; if there is more than one, (e.g., TV and fireplace or TV and a special view) it gets a bit complicated, but is still very doable. I usually ask my clients what their priority is and how they spend their free time together. If people enjoy and use the fireplace often while watching TV, it is best to put the TV closer to the fireplace like in Diagram 11. This way, you can combine focal points and have a comfortable sitting area around it. You can put the TV in the closest corner to the fireplace or have the TV above the fireplace. Make sure the TV is not too high, otherwise it might be strenuous on your neck. If there is no way to lower the TV, you can move the sofa away from the TV/fireplace wall if the space allows.

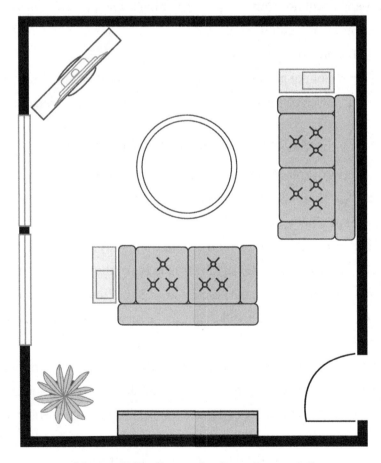

Diagram 11: Family room furniture placement—1

In case you do have a special view and want to have a TV in your family room, you can place the TV in the corner adjacent to the window with the view.

Earlier in Chapter 5, we talked about the importance of having comfortable sofas and chairs.

The sofa is one of the most used pieces of furniture, so spend some time learning your options and make sure it is comfortable and fits well in your room. It's best if you test it in person and sit on it before you buy it. Some people like it cushy and soft, some prefer medium, and not too many like hard sofas.

Sometimes I hear from clients that they didn't test their sofa well enough, and it's uncomfortable. At times, they even say they hate it. But they still keep it, although it irritates them and reminds them every day that they've made a mistake. I suggest you bite the bullet and get rid of it. Otherwise, not only will you be uncomfortable and avoid using it, but there will also always be an underlying feeling of self-blame for the mistake.

The sofa has to be the right size and height. It also has to be the right depth for you. You must pay attention to the side rest. Some of them are cushier and more rounded, and some are pretty hard and straight and cannot be used as an armrest.

Since the sofa is a large piece, the color matters too. White or other very light-colored sofas are beautiful, but if you have animals and young kids, you most likely will regret it if you buy a light-colored sofa. Very dark ones often are not ideal either, especially black ones, as it will create a large dark area in the room. Great sofa colors are somewhere in the middle like cappuccino, light chocolate, or some warm gray shades.

Make sure it is not the same color as your rug or walls, otherwise you will have a boring, monochromatic environment.

If you use a sofa to separate spaces, it is better if the sofa has a straight back rather than a slanted back. Also, the sofa's back should not be too high or too low. If it is too high, it will block the other room too much, and if it is too low, you will feel that your back is unprotected.

To create a sitting area, you either need to use two sofas, one L-shaped sofa and a chair, or one sofa and two chairs. If you have a choice, do not place a second sofa by the window. In Diagram 12 we arranged the sitting area around the TV, and we placed the sofa by the solid wall behind it to be able to enjoy the view. Note that it is best not to sit with your back directly to the door. We avoided this situation in both arrangements.

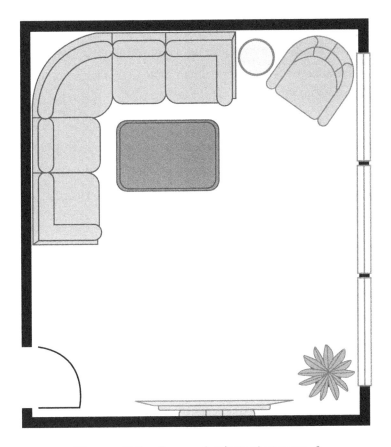

Diagram 12: Family room furniture placement—2

A rug is a wonderful addition to your family room décor. It makes the room warmer, softer, and therefore more comfortable. It also absorbs sound. For best results, allow the rug to encompass all the furniture of your sitting area and to separate it from the rest of your room, especially if it is an open floor concept or a very large room. A round rug sometimes works well because it creates a soft entrance into the room rather than entering at the corner of a square or rectangular rug.

A coffee table provides convenience and comfort in every family room. If you like to put your legs up while watching TV, you may want to consider a leather cocktail ottoman instead of a hardwood surface. I am not a big fan of glass coffee tables. The surface is too hard and cold, and they are harder to keep clean.

Bookshelves or built-in cabinets create surfaces to place family photos, some travel trophies, and other family mementos. All those things in the right amount and placed properly help to create a feeling of happiness.

Family Room Lighting

The lighting in the family room should accommodate various activities and be adaptable for different times of the day. It is best if the family room has different types of lighting that you can switch to depending on the time of the day and the activity.

The ambient or general lighting is usually provided by recessed lighting or a combination of recessed lighting and a chandelier. Cove lighting works well in the family room, providing uniform light that bounces off the ceiling. If the ceiling has beautiful architectural details, it could also draw your attention to it.

Torchiere floor lamps that direct light toward the ceiling are also used to provide ambient lighting. They can be used as a source of warmer or more yellow-colored lighting in the evening.

Track lighting or angled recessed lighting can be used for illuminating a beautiful architectural detail, a piece of art, or bookshelves with special accessories and family photos.

Table lamps on side tables provide a more intimate form of lighting and are beautiful additions to your room. A reading lamp can brighten your favorite spot in the room for curling up with a book.

Family Room Art

The best kind of art in the family room is the art that has some meaning for you and your family. Whether you have expensive pieces of art, or your own photos, it will work well for you and your family if your art has an association with special landscapes, seascapes, places you've been and had some good times at, or places where you want to be. In my family room, we have pictures that I took or bought in Hawaii, which is a very special place for my husband and me. The pictures bring memories filled with adventure, sun, relaxation, and fun. Even when I do not consciously think about it, it creates comfort in my subconscious mind and a sense of happiness.

I am not a big fan of abstract art in a family room, especially because it doesn't have much emotion in it, but that could just be me. It might be different for you. This is why I invite you to ask yourself what kind of feeling it brings when you tune into each piece. If it makes you feel joyful, comfortable, expanded, uplifted, or positive in any other way, then it is a good piece for you. If it makes you feel contracted, cold, or negative in any other way, then pass on this piece; it will not do any good for you.

You can use art to balance the Five Elements. If any Element is missing, it is easy to add it in the form of artwork. Please refer to the beginning of this chapter for examples of the Five Elements in art. There are guidelines in Chapter 7 on the size of the artwork and hanging art above the sofa.

Do not place images of Water above the fireplace. Water above Fire creates an elemental clash that might sometimes be experienced as disharmony between family members.

Family Room Accessories

The family room is a good place to display a few of your family photos.

Other great accessories include beautiful ceramic or clay items, woodwork, or metalwork. Displaying something of different cultures that you brought back from your travels is a plus because it will have the energy of those places. But beware of displaying indigenous items or any kind of religious or ceremonial items whose usage and particular energy you don't understand. Some things do not belong in your home. Use your judgment.

Sometimes kids' art and your own art can be special and worth displaying. Just don't fall into the trap that you need to display all the pieces that your kids have ever created. If there are too many things, our mind stops processing them individually and gets overwhelmed. Every item, depending on the size and strength of its presence, should have some space around it, otherwise it will get lost in the clutter.

Although, at times, you can find something really nice for less money, most of the time I am not a big fan of the random interior design items that Pier One or Home Goods are overfilled with. Because the merchandise in these stores is pretty inexpensive, people end up with way too many things. Seek meaningful decorations that speak to your heart and soul to surround yourself with, and remember the "less is more" rule.

Family Room Talismans and Special Objects

Natural crystals like rose quartz chunks, white quartz clusters, amethyst, and celestine emanate strong earth energy, are beautiful, and can fill the space with a positive vibration.

Rose quartz brings calm, a heartfelt feeling, and joy to the space, while a white quartz cluster brings purity and a soft, healing energy. I am most familiar with these two and use them often. There is a whole world of natural crystals, and if you know quite a bit about them and are attracted to some of them, use those in your family room, by all means. At times, I see people love natural crystals so much that they have multiple collections of them throughout the house. Like with everything else, if there is too much of it, it becomes cluttered. Rather than having them in every room, have one, two, or a maximum of three areas where you display them. A few large pieces are better than multiple small pieces.

Family Room Plants

If the room is large, consider placing a taller tree. Placing an ivy plant on a shelf and letting it flow on the side of the shelf will soften its sharp edges. If there is a low window or a wide window seal, it is an excellent place for some plants in pots. Plant stands with beautiful pots and plants on them can be a great addition to your family room décor.

> *People report that after completing their family room by*
> *following these guidelines, they experience more closeness*
> *with their family, more harmony, and more happiness.*
> *Some people even say that they see change in their teenage*
> *children. The ones who typically try to spend as little time*
> *with their parents as possible suddenly want to hang out*
> *more in the family room with the rest of the family.*

Now let's shift our focus to what may be the most important room in the house: the bedroom.

CHAPTER 14

The Bedroom

The bedroom represents our inner self and our relationship and is likely the most important room in our home. Recent studies compared the three biggest aspects of our existence, such as financial security, supportive relationships, and good sleep, and came up with the unexpected result that good sleep is more important to our well-being and health than finances and relationships! I think we can't really compare ourselves to some kind of average person and the importance of these aspects will vary from person to person, but you get the idea—sleep (and, therefore, the bedroom) is important.

> *If the bedroom is well organized, simple, nourishing, and energetically clean, you will be able to sleep better and deeper.*

This statement has been proven in my practice numerous times.

The two main functions of the bedroom are sleep and relating to each other in an intimate way or making love. It is a big mistake to bring other functions, especially work, into your bedroom. It is understandable that when people have a small home with only a few rooms, they will be tempted to put a desk in their bedroom. Inevitably, it will create stress and deplete your sleep. You have to be creative in a small home, and it would be better to put your desk in the corner of your living room rather than the bedroom.

If you have a choice, the best location for the master bedroom is at the back of the house, away from the street where it is quieter and there is a view of a peaceful nature. In city apartments, the best bedroom location is also away from the busiest street. For children's rooms or a guest bedroom, it is fine to be located at the busier or noisier part of the house.

Our energy is most open and sensitive during sleep. Since the bedroom is the room where we spend a third of our life, the environment has to be supportive of our personal energy, especially the energy of the heart.

The bedroom is your private, personal haven. The room should totally represent your sensitive, quiet self, not the person you are in social settings or at work. It should represent the real you that is underneath all the responsibilities and duties. Both women and men have this private, sensitive inner part.

If you have a partner, I suggest including him or her in the bedroom design decisions too. When we are in a harmonious relationship, often there is something in common between the energies of two people—certain qualities will be similar and present in both of them. This something you have in common should be reflected in your bedroom's design. It could be that you both want to create in the space a feeling of softness and sensuality or playfulness and passion or stability and joy. If you and your partner want different things, then what's acceptable and pleasing to both of you should be carefully negotiated. If you are single and open to a new relationship, then you may want to incorporate into your bedroom the elements of décor that help to create feelings and qualities that you want to have in a happy and nourishing relationship. On the next pages, we will discuss how to do this with colors, art, and accessories.

Way too often, I see that the bedroom is the last room people attend to. All the rest of the house will be remodeled and beautifully designed, but the bedroom is left to the end, and it may take years to come back to it and finish. When I see this pattern, I know that the person is not taking good care of themselves. The outer appearance and what others think is more important to them than their own needs. This might be a sign that we are not confident enough. This might give us a clue that we don't know how to take care of ourselves and address our needs. When I talk to people about it, they really want to do it, but they have a tendency to put their personal needs last. In fact, many don't really know what they want. It takes time to change this pattern, but redesigning your bedroom and giving something to yourself like a new bed, a new mattress, or a special piece of art will speed things up for you a great deal in this area.

Make the process of designing your bedroom one of self-discovery and finding your joy again. Your bedroom can be a place that supports this process of coming back home to yourself. It could be a process of trying different things, different colors, and art to see what gives you this quiet feeling of fullness, belonging, and satisfaction.

Yin/Yang and the Five Elements in the Bedroom

The bedroom will feel the most restful and comfortable if more yin elements are implemented in the design than yang elements.

Yin: darker, more soothing or softer wall colors, soft throw blanket, soft rugs, relaxing images, soft light.

Yang: bright, saturated or white colors; mirrors, a TV, sharp architectural details, beams, hard floors, disturbing art or geometrical images, bright lights.

Wood Element in the form of small plants, soft pastel green colors, or a wooden bed will bring natural elements and a sense of vitality.

Fire Element should be used in moderation in bedrooms; however, **yin Fire** of pink colors or images of flowers are excellent in bedrooms.

Earth Element is very appropriate in bedrooms. Earthy colors and images of flowering fields have calming and nourishing qualities.

Metal Element such as pure white walls or sharp and large metal accessories are not appropriate in bedrooms. White sheets or a white rug would bring a sense of purity and cleanliness.

Water Element is appropriate in the form of a blue color and organic wavy patterns in curtains, rugs, or bedding. Art depicting water brings a sense of relaxation and happy vacation memories. Water fountains are not appropriate in bedrooms.

Bedroom Color

Because our energy is more sensitive in the bedroom, I never recommend using intense colors there. I learned my lesson when, years ago, at the beginning of my feng shui career, I worked with a husband and wife who were in their mid-fifties and wanted to energize their relationship. I mentioned that using some elements of red in their bedroom would help them to bring more passion to their love life. I mentioned art with reds, a bedspread with a red floral pattern, or just a red throw blanket.

When I came back for a follow-up in a year, they reported that there was definitely more energy in their love life, but their sleep got worse, and they argued way more than before. When I saw the bedroom, I understood why. The bedroom walls were dark red! They said they liked the idea that red would bring more passion and thought the more the merrier. After that I always carry color samples with me and try to come up with an exact color for the rooms that need paint. My clients repainted their bedroom with a more gentle and subtle yet beautiful and inspiring pinkish purplish tone and reported more harmony in their relationship and improved sleep. I would not recommend using any intense or bold colors from the Fire family in the bedroom. And I would not use pure white in the bedroom either. White is somewhat harsh, cold, and unemotional for bedrooms.

Soft and warm earthy colors work best in bedrooms. They are pretty close to neutral, but the trick here is to use neutral colors that have some amount of actual color in them. If you look at the color wheel, there are many shades in between the saturated colors and most neutral colors. Look at those that are close to neutral but have some small amount of color in them. These shades are not loud, but they are also not flat and boring like your typical beige, cream, white, or gray. Consider muted sage green or muted warm blue—this will make the room feel relaxing and grounded, yet alive.

My favorite color in the master bedroom is pink. There is a class of pinks that I call "adult pink." They might be close to mauves, but I don't think they are exactly mauves. They are earthy tones but with some small amount of pink in them. You can find the exact colors that I am trying to describe here in the complimentary e-book, which you can find in the Shop section on my website, www.nataliakaylin.com. They invoke a calm, nourishing, and happy feeling in the heart. Most people respond to these shades beautifully because they feel that the color does something positive to them. Many people feel happy, open, and relaxed when they are surrounded by these soft, earthy colors with a touch of pink in them.

Surprisingly, most men respond to them as well as women. I didn't expect that men would respond positively to them when I first started using them, but now it is no surprise to me. These are my client's words after they painted their bedroom in adult pink: "My husband is responding in a surprisingly positive fashion. He told me that when he walks into our bedroom, he just smiles, and yesterday he said, 'I am just so happy here.'"

If painting your bedroom walls with an "adult pink" is not an option, you will still benefit from using some throw blankets, pillows, or art in this family of colors.

Some people prefer purple or lilac to pink, but make sure to choose one with warmer tones. These purple spectrum colors do not work on the heart the same way pinks do, but they are very calming and pleasing to the eye and, if combined with green accents, may bring a sense of youthfulness and spring, which is quite appropriate in a bedroom.

Often it is a good idea to paint the wall behind the bed a shade or two darker than the rest of the walls. This will bring the feeling of being grounded at the headboard's wall. Also, a more saturated shade of a color you love will help to create more beauty and a positive response.

Choosing the right color is a big step toward creating a soulful bedroom. If multiple color choices speak to you, then you should paint a few samples on the wall and feel which one is helping to create an emotion that you want to feel. If you want to bring a sense of relaxation, nourishment, youthfulness, or love, find the color that carries the frequencies of these feelings. I hope some of these recommendations will speak to you; if not, experiment until you find the color that feels just right for you.

Bedroom Furniture

Your bed could easily be the most important piece of furniture in your entire house. There are many different bed styles, shapes, and materials. Here are some guidelines that will help you choose a good bed for you.

The bed should hold and support your body in the most comfortable way. A wooden bed frame with a solid wooden headboard is your best choice. A solid headboard provides support and protection for your head and body. The bed should be sturdy, and the headboard should be attached well so it doesn't move around. Without a headboard, your bed's location is perceived as temporary and not grounded enough. This could negatively impact both your ability to get restful sleep and your relationship.

I have seen plenty of single people, men and women, whose bed doesn't have a solid headboard. There are two problems with a headboard that has holes or slats. First, it doesn't hold the energy, therefore you don't feel as relaxed and comfortable as you could be; second, it might introduce too much sharp energy by your head. Your second best choice is an upholstered fabric or leather headboard. The reason the wood is better is that in the upholstered headboard they use materials that typically will off-gas for some period of time. Some people report being affected by it, and often, if the materials are cheap, you can smell it in the bedroom for a few months. In terms of off-gassing, you should be careful with any piece of furniture you bring into the bedroom. You spend more time in this room than any other, and your energy is more open in the bedroom, so you are more sensitive and susceptible to negative (and positive too!) influences.

The bed should be not too high or too low. If it is too high, it is uncomfortable. If it is too low, it doesn't allow energy to circulate freely under the bed which, with time, will create a stagnation. Stagnating energy under the bed will eventually start draining your energy. This is the reason for not having storage boxes under your bed. Also, you will not be able to vacuum under the bed if there is stuff there or if the frame is too low, which will also contribute to stagnation. Additionally, dust may contribute to allergies in some people.

Metal beds are not desirable because metal is a conductive material and may amplify any small electromagnetic currents that may come from the earth and underground water. There are some energies that are not compatible with our human system, and it is best not to amplify them. Metal headboards are not solid, and energy leaks through them. In addition, metal beds are cold and hard to the touch.

The mattress is another big piece to be aware of and definitely needs to be researched before you buy it. I know several people whose health diminished after they bought a new mattress. Typically these people's immune system are not strong and they have other chemical sensitivities or allergies. Unfortunately, the rule here is the less money you pay for a mattress, the more probability that it will have some toxic materials in it, and these materials can be released into the air. Having an air purifier in your bedroom helps to reduce these materials, and so does opening the windows.

It is best to have two nightstands—one on each side of the bed and a lamp on each of them—whether you are married or single. This way both partners are equally represented and, for a single person, there is a positive message about partnership, if this is something that you want.

Dressers should be proportional to the size of the bed. Make sure that there is enough space between the dresser and the bed. If you feel cramped, move the dresser to a different wall.

Mirrors, especially large ones, are not advisable in bedrooms. They create active and unrestful energy in bedrooms. Besides, it can be spooky to see yourself in the mirror at night. It's best to place a mirror in a closet. If there is no space in the closet, then hang a mirror on the inside of the closet door. If you like a full-length mirror in your bedroom, place it so you don't see yourself in the mirror from the bed.

The bedroom is the only room where wall-to-wall carpet makes some sense, especially if you can install a natural wool carpet. If you have a hardwood floor, place a rug for comfort and softness. I like slightly off-white soft shag or wool rugs that go all the way under the bed and on both sides of the bed.

The bedroom is not a good place for bookshelves, TVs, desks, or sofas. If your bedroom is too large, place a couple of chairs or a loveseat so the room is not so empty or place a screen or curtain to create some separation from the bedroom and create your meditation area. All the other furniture will bring too much of a different kind of energy that is not compatible with rest and good sleep. If you don't have any other choice and must have your work desk in your bedroom, you should also use a screen or create some kind of separation between your bed and desk. Also, you will sleep better if you turn off your laptop and other electronic devices completely.

It's a good practice not to have a TV in the bedroom as the things we watch, especially news, bring chaos and unrest into a sensitive area where you are trying to unwind and rest. The same goes with all electronic devices. Electronics are a big contributor to the quality of sleep. The fewer pieces of electronics you have in a bedroom, the better you will sleep. Recent studies suggest you should not look at the TV, computer, or cell phone screens at least thirty minutes before your sleep time. The screens emanate blue light, which decreases the production of melatonin and screws up your circadian rhythms, preventing you from getting a deep sleep. Yes, you can switch your screens to more yellow light or even purchase yellow-light glasses, but it is not only the color of the light that influences us, but the electromagnetic fields (EMFs) that all devices emanate. Definitely do not have your cell phone or tablet on your nightstand and especially do not have chargers plugged into the wall behind your head or close to your head.

Shades are especially advisable in a bedroom. Research shows sleep improvement in totally dark rooms. I personally use 80 percent darkening shades because I like to see if it is morning or still night by just glancing at the shades rather than an alarm clock. I personally am not a big fan of curtains because I love to have all the light from the windows I can get and curtains often reduce light quite a bit. Fabric shades, however, are perfect, because when they fold, they do not obstruct any light. You can choose them in a neutral color or can bring some color for fun. Wooden shades are not soft enough for bedrooms. If you have an artistic touch, you can play with fabric curtains. Sometimes they can be quite special and bring softness, beauty, and other good qualities.

If you have an obsession for comfort and are like me, I want to invite you to indulge different senses in the bedroom. Create a soft and sensual atmosphere where besides visual senses, your touch sense can be indulged by the softness of a rug or sheepskin, the silkiness of sheets, and the fuzziness of a throw blanket. After all, more than half of the time we experience the bedroom in the semidarkness, which makes touch one of the main senses in the bedroom.

The Bed Placement and Energy Flow

The quality of your sleep will depend on the placement of the bed in the room. Some areas of the room will have more restful and supportive energy, and others will have more active and dispersed energy. For the best results, energy should not move too fast at the bed location; rather, it should accumulate there in a nourishing way. To best support your essential energies, have a solid wall behind your head. Although it is not always possible to implement, take a look at the ideal bed placement illustrated in Diagram 13. It is best if the bed is placed diagonally from the bedroom entrance with the headboard at the wall that doesn't have windows or doors. You should not see too much of the bathroom and especially not the toilet from your bed.

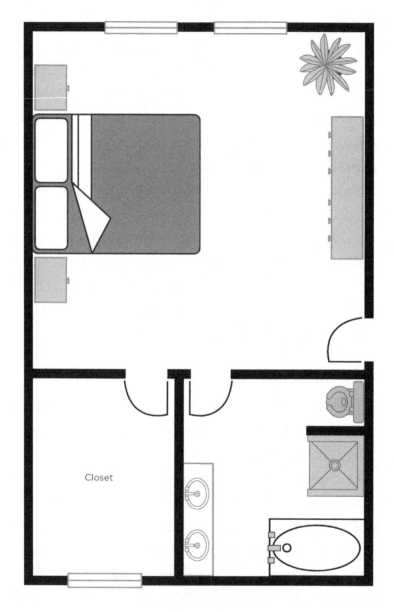

Diagram 13: Bedroom furniture placement

Closet

Make sure that on the other side of the wall where your head is you don't have a TV, computer, or other electronic equipment. Electromagnetic radiation (EMR) travels through the walls. It doesn't happen too often, but some of my clients had an electrical distribution panel in the wall right next to their head, and others were sleeping right above the electrical distribution panel in their basement. All of the people who were affected by EMR have experienced headaches, disturbed sleep, and fatigue at the minimum. When they moved their beds, 100 percent of them felt better, some of them within days, others within weeks. To move away from an area of high EMR would be a priority, even if you have to break all the rest of the feng shui rules!

Bedroom Lighting

In some bedrooms a chandelier or a ceiling pendant can be used as a source of ambient lighting, but lighting near the bed might be just enough. A chandelier in a bedroom is more of an aesthetic feature, but the lighting near the bed is a necessity. If you choose to have a chandelier, make sure it doesn't have any sharp features and edges but rather is soft and round and exudes a harmonious feeling, as this is something you will see from the bed. Sometimes people combine ceiling fans that have lights. Try to avoid ceiling fans altogether in the bedroom, especially for rooms with lower ceilings as fans are sharp, bulky, and often feel oppressive seen from the bed. Find other ways to cool off and circulate air in the room.

If you like to read in bed, then your best lighting choice is to have two wall-mounted light fixtures with adjustable arms so that the light can be directed on your book.

Table lamps on nightstands with warm-colored shades are a good way to provide a soft mood or reading lighting in the bedroom. Remember, exposure to the red, orange, and yellow part of the light spectrum is correlated to production of melatonin (sleeping hormone). Of course, don't use bright red- or orange-colored shades, but some earthy toned-down shades might be a good choice. Definitely use yellow-spectrum light bulbs, not white or blue ones. It is also useful to have your bedroom lighting on a dimmer.

Bedroom Art

Before we fall asleep and right when we wake up, we are in a special and sensitive state where we are influenced the most by the things around us. This is why we need to consider bedroom art carefully. Something soft, beautiful, and meaningful would work best here. For example, flowers that touch you by their beauty or sensuality or a soft landscape, especially if it is a vacation spot that reminds you of a happy and relaxing time.

If you are married, or have a partner, it is best if the piece of art is meaningful for both partners. Whether you are in a relationship or not, the bedroom is an excellent place to display art that represents love. And the images that touch us and reflect how we want to feel are different for everyone. It doesn't matter whether you are a man or a woman, whether you are already happily married or still looking to fulfill this important aspect of your life, it is our inherent, deep need to love and be loved. To find out what will work best for you, I suggest this exercise.

Close your eyes, take a few deep breaths, and let yourself remember a time when you were in love. Place your awareness in the middle of your chest and allow yourself to be flooded with the feeling. At first you may feel the person you were with, but eventually let go of the person and feel *you*. It is *your* feeling, it is *your* ability to feel love.

Ask yourself these simple questions: *What are the qualities that are present in my heart and my body right now? How does being loved make me feel?* Some of the qualities might be: open, flowing, tingling, uplifted, relaxed, excited, strong, etc. Notice a few of the strongest qualities. Then ask yourself, *How do I want to feel when I am with my loved one? For example, do I want to have a passionate and exciting love, or do I prefer a soft and caring love?*

Animals and flowers are more subtle than dancing couples and can project a beautiful emotion of caring, sensuality, and tenderness. Tenderness and care can be felt in a pair of birds. Two sensual flowers are often a winner for a piece of art above the bed. A pair of white horses can project a great deal of passion and sensuality. But if nothing works better for you than an image of a happy couple, go for it!

Besides expressions of love, any peaceful, beautiful image that touches you and brings joy is welcome in the bedroom. If you are happily married, pictures of the two of you are great in the bedroom, especially pictures from happy travels and some special moments together. Pictures of children or parents do not belong in the bedroom. It's weird to see your children's faces while making love. Even more weird to have your parents "watching you."

Bedroom Accessories

The fewer things we have in the bedroom, the better our sleep is. See more about decluttering in Chapter 3.

A picture or two of you and your loving partner on your dresser and a special jewelry box are the few things that are nice to have in a bedroom.

Bedroom Plants

I like living plants in every room, including my bedroom. I have a plumeria in my bedroom that blooms most of the year and creates a heavenly, sweet scent. As I mentioned earlier, I like to indulge all my senses in my bedroom, and this includes scent. Plumeria is a flower used in garlands in Hawaii, and when I close my eyes I feel I am being transported to the Big Island of Hawaii, my favorite place on Earth. Orchids are such pure and beautiful creatures; they bring beauty to every bedroom.

Bedroom Altars

If you want to attract a new partner or honor and strengthen your current relationship, you can take one step further and create a relationship altar. For people who are in a relationship, the altar can consist of a picture of both of you and a piece of rose quartz, either a heart-shaped one or just an unpolished piece. Rose quartz is a stone that has vibrations that influence the heart in a very positive way. Some say it is a love stone. You can certainly add any other object to your altar that represents love to you. Your altar is very personal, and it has to resonate with you. Choose a picture where you are happy. It could be a spontaneous shot taken during the time you were genuinely happy and relaxed rather than a photographer-posed picture, although those can be happy too. If your wedding was a special and happy event, you may want to display a photo of it too. Be aware that, for some people, their wedding was stressful.

Julia's Story

My client Julia was in her fifties, had two adult sons, and had been divorced for a while when she decided that she was ready for a new relationship. She got inspired after our meeting and changed her entire bedroom set, which was from her previous marriage, including the mattress. And since her bed didn't have a solid headboard, she decided to treat herself to a new bed. She removed all of her beautiful, but very sad, art pieces that resonated with her own sadness. Being an artistic person, she took some pictures of paired birds and put them in her newly painted bedroom.

When I came back for a follow-up, she reported increased activity in her dating. She was excited but still hadn't met someone she would be able to trust and love. This is when I suggested she create an altar that represented what kind of love she wanted in her life. From another room, she brought a small side table that her yoga student (a craftsman) made for her with lots of care. On it, she arranged two special candles decorated with cherry blossoms, a hand-drawn picture of a heart, and an orchid. All together, her arrangement emanated care, trust, depth, spring, and pure joy.

Soon after she put her altar together, she met someone on a dating site. It was quite a miracle because he had only used the site for a short time and went online to close his account that day because he thought it was not for him. A few days after they connected, he flew across the country to meet her. It was instant love and acceptance on both sides. He treated her like she was his princess, and he still does fifteen years later. Yes, you can start all over again in your fifties, sixties, or seventies and be happy and loved; you just need to meet the right person.

I hope your relationship with your bedroom will change forever, and you may even prioritize its design now.

Now, our journey continues to the children's rooms.

CHAPTER 15

Children's Rooms

A child's room is a world to them, and it is up to us to bring the support and structure they need along with all the beautiful things that inspire imagination, curiosity, fascination, and attention.

> *One of our biggest desires is for our children to thrive and do well in the world. Creating safe and nourishing spaces for them will not only help with their sleep and study, but will also contribute to their confidence, creativity, vitality, and happiness.*

Children's energy and their needs are somewhat different from ours. It's good to understand and address their emotional disposition so we can give them the specific support they need. When I work with a child's room, I ask questions about their personality, behavior, their level of vitality, and their overall happiness.

In addition to the parents' answers, I can get a good read from the room itself. Over the years, I have seen correlations between children's environments and their personalities, and I have learned how to correct some behavioral and emotional patterns by changing their environment. Shy children need a very different kind of support than overly active children. Children who have trouble concentrating need even more specific support from their environment.

> *Often parents report improvements in their children's school performance and ability to concentrate after we move their desk as well as improved sleep after we find a better placement for their bed. Adding the right colors helps to support and balance a child's energy and their emotional states.*

Babies' and young children's rooms are always special to see, feel, and work with. Many parents put a lot of care and time into creating a room for their baby, especially their first one. All the gorgeous wall colors and decals, beautiful little furniture, and accessories help to create a special atmosphere of a safe haven and joy.

Teenager's rooms vary a great deal. It is quite easy for me to feel a teenager's personality by just looking at their room. I can feel whether they are shy, confident, happy, balanced, angry, rebellious, or depressed. Often parents whose children are not easy ask me for help after exhausting other resources.

Daniella's Story

Daniella was fourteen when I consulted for her parents' home. It was a beautiful, tastefully decorated suburban home. When I saw Daniella's pink room with charming fairy tale princess white furniture, I thought it was the room of a five-year-old girl. I was pretty surprised, and her mom explained that she didn't allow Daniella to make any changes.

I could feel that Olivia loved her daughter very much, but she was quite a perfectionist and didn't trust that Daniella would make the "right choices" decorating her room. Besides, Olivia said that she was uncomfortable with "all of the teenage stuff," and so she thought that she was "protecting [her] daughter from all of this." I explained how important it was for Daniella to express who she was now and to make her own choices and suggested that Olivia allow Daniella to make some changes, at least to start by hanging a few posters that would represent something that a fourteen-year-old was passionate about.

A year later I was called back, and this time I met Daniella. Her room was still the same; nothing had changed. It came up in conversation that she doesn't perceive herself as a creative person and doesn't quite know what she likes. Olivia was taken by surprise but immediately understood what had happened. She said, "Oh my God, it is totally my fault, we have to do something now!" Daniella's confession helped Olivia to understand that she went too far trying to control and protect her daughter.

We started to discuss colors and furniture options, and Daniella started to get more and more interested in it and excited about the possibility of making changes. Quite spontaneously, she started to come up with some pretty good ideas. I didn't give Daniella too many guidelines, emphasizing that it was good for her to try things and it was totally okay to make mistakes.

I have not had a chance to follow up with this family, but I do hope the "spell" that Daniella wasn't creative and capable to design her own space was broken, and that having a chance to design her room gave her a chance to perceive herself as a creative and capable person, especially when the time comes for her to have her own space.

So many times I have observed in others and myself that the fear of making mistakes cripples our creativity and limits the flow of ideas and possibilities. It is a gift to our children to give them gentle support and provide them with opportunities to express themselves and learn from their mistakes and accomplishments.

Children's Rooms Colors

Having two or three different colors next to each other creates contrast. Contrast creates energy and liveliness, which is generally great in kids' rooms, but be aware that too much contrast will create too much energy. Spaces with too little contrast are more relaxing but can be too disengaging. So choose according to your child's needs. If you feel like they need to be energized more, create contrast with more saturated colors, and if they need to be pacified, use pastel tones with less contrast. Examples of strong contrast are red and blue, orange and green, or red and yellow.

Examples of gentler contrast are pink and green, pink and white, yellow and green, or green and blue. It also depends on the shade and level of saturation of a particular color.

Often a child knows what wall color they want, and it is good for their sense of developing self to get what they want. But sometimes their choices can be pretty random or disturbing. Occasionally, I see that a room is way too bright or way too dark. We can make some educated suggestions and see if they can relate to it. If we do it in a noncontrolling manner, children will go with it.

I remember one case with a seriously depressed thirteen-year-old boy who had a very dark green room with black curtains and some pretty disturbing posters. His mom said he requested to paint his room a dark color and despite her hesitation, she helped him with painting it a few years earlier.

She mentioned that "He wants to paint the walls black now." I explained that her son created an environment that reflected his emotional state, and no matter how much therapy he was doing, his condition would hardly improve because the environment where he spent a lot of time was depleting and depressing.

Often it is hard to convince teenagers to make any changes in their room, but this was the case where I asked to insist. I suggested light and warm green walls to infuse the boy with healing and balancing vibrations, a light brown rug for stability, yellow pillows for cheerfulness, and a blue comforter and window shades for calmness. I found out that the boy likes cars and suggested he find some car posters and let him choose a few as part of his room redo. This helped to get rid of the disturbing posters and surround him with something more positive. A few months later, the mother emailed me saying that there were noticeable improvements in her son's health and emotional levels.

Here are some wall color guidelines for children that I've used over the years with great success:

- ▶ If your child is shy and reserved, he or she would benefit from a more stimulating environment. Go with brighter and warmer wall colors such as yellow, pink, or green. Although, be careful with yellow. Some shades are overly bright and stimulating, and it is hard to live with them.

- ▶ If your child is hyperactive and having trouble falling asleep, lighter and colder colors are a better choice such as warm blue, soft green, very light pink, or lilac.

- ▶ If your child is confident, balanced, and grounded, you don't need to limit them in color choices. Usually they make the right choice.

- ▶ If a child has trouble concentrating, do not use too bright or contrasting color schemes. It is important not to overwhelm and overstimulate their senses; therefore, keeping things simple, clean, and spacious would be best. It's very important to help them create a good organization system.

Most children intuitively make good color choices. One thing I sometimes see from working with children directly is that they go with a brighter color because they just don't know that if you apply the saturated color to the wall, the color will look brighter and therefore more intense, which often is too much. I help children to find the color they like in a more toned-down and softer version of the same color. For most children, blue, green, pink, lilac, or yellow would be a great choice. The colors that adults are attracted to, which are gray, white, beige, or tan don't have enough energy in them for a child's room.

Contrast wall colors with colors of the rugs, comforter covers, and wall art. For example, if the wall colors are pink, use whites and greens with it. If the wall colors are green, use pinks or yellows with it. If the wall colors are blue, yellow, or red, accents create a beautiful contrast.

Children's Rooms Bed Placement

The best bed for children, just like for adults, is made of wood and with a solid headboard, either wood or upholstered. A solid wall behind the headboard will add additional support. For older children, bed placement can be similar to the adults' bed-placement guidelines. It is placed diagonally from the door with a view of the windows.

For younger children, it is best to place their bed by the wall. They will feel more protected and supported if the bed is placed in the corner of the room. It's often hard to place the bed along the wall because of the windows. Make sure to find a corner that has more wall space and fewer windows.

Many boys love bunk beds, and they are fun when friends are sleeping over, but they are actually quite terrible. The top one creates visual and energetic pressure for a child sleeping in the lower one, so there might be a feeling of confinement. The top one is simply dangerous because a child can fall at any time during the night. It really does happen. I would avoid bunk beds even if you have a small room with two children in it and try to find an optimal place for both beds.

If your child is school age, you may need to add a desk to their room. It is often quite a challenge to find a good place for a bed and a desk in the same room. You need to be really creative with it, and if at all possible, place the desk in a way that a child would have an open space in front of them and a wall behind their back, which is rarely possible due to the constraints of the space. Facing a window or having a window on the side is good, but many children end up facing a wall while sitting at their desk.

If this is the case, consider placing a photo of nature that has an openness in it like an ocean or a meadow. Research shows that seeing nature helps children and adults who have trouble concentrating. I think seeing nature makes us happier and more relaxed but not sleepy, which in turn allows better concentration and productivity. Having an open space in front of us correlates with increased creativity.

You may want to minimize the view of the bed. If a child sees the bed, they will be less productive and feel sleepy. Inevitably, they end up sitting or lying on the bed engaging with their social media friends rather than with their homework.

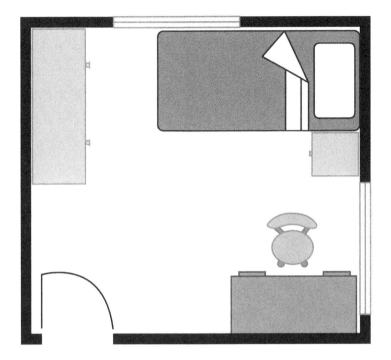

Diagram 14: Children's room furniture placement

The material and size of the desk matters. Metal or glass are not good materials for adult or children's desks. Wood is best. The size should not be too small, otherwise your child will feel constricted. I think four feet should be the minimum desk length. It should not be too big either.

Make sure there are no sharp objects pointing at the child's head while they are in bed or sitting at their desk. This includes shelves, bookcases, and edges of dressers. Some children have headboards that have shelves right behind them, and there are all kinds of things pointing at their heads and collecting dust.

Like with adult bedrooms, the same goes with electronic devices in children's bedrooms. Children are even more sensitive to EMR than adults. I had a case of a young girl who was sleeping for thirteen years right above the electrical panel in the basement. The electrical wiring insulation was leaking at the top of the panel, and the level of EMR was high at the child's bed where her head was. She slept poorly, had low energy, headaches, food sensitivities, and this wasn't even the full list of her health and emotional problems. After the bed was moved away from the EMR source, she changed pretty dramatically, and two years later when I met her again, she played sports, her grades had improved, and she was relaxed, confident, and happy.

Often children will resist the change at first, but after they try it, they usually like it. After we worked in the room of a ten-year-old boy, his mother emailed me: "After you left I had to tell my son that we were moving his bed and his desk. He was not happy, but now I can't tell you how happy he is with the change. He keeps saying, 'I love my new bedroom!' He is definitely sleeping more soundly and longer than before. I can't believe I didn't look into this earlier." Some years later, he said that he was always super aware of his surroundings and tried to create supportive spaces for himself.

Children's Rooms Lighting

Children's rooms need to be bright and cheerful, therefore they need a good amount of ambient lighting. Often a chandelier is used in combination with a floor torchiere lamp. If your child does their homework in their room, make sure to provide them with a task lamp. You can get an LED table or floor lamp online with different settings for different tasks and different color lighting for working in the evenings and during the day. If your child likes to read in bed, they will need a good reading lamp, either on the nightstand or an adjustable-arm light fixture. Lanterns can be used for creating a special story-like atmosphere in one of the corners of the room. Chandeliers and lampshades can be great fun and art pieces of their own kind.

Children's Rooms Art

As I mentioned earlier, children's rooms are a world to them, and we can bring magic into it by helping them to choose some beautiful images that stimulate their senses and imagination. There was no children's art in my childhood home, but I still remember when I slept at my grandmother's house, the guest room had a wall rug with a colorful and exotic flamenco dance scene. Before I fell asleep, I spent some time thinking about these passionate and freedom-loving women and men, imagining their lives. The scene was so different from the environment I was growing up in. I am pretty sure that image planted in me a seed of a desire to travel the world and experience these colorful and passionate southern cultures.

These days, many beautiful images are available for our children's enjoyment. I think especially good ones are pictures of magical creatures and animals, wall decals, or stickers of nature; anything you can imagine and more is available to support your child's curiosity, creativity, and imagination. If your child is not too little, ask their opinion, of course, if they like it or want it in their room.

Children's Rooms Accessories and Toys

Children in Western society have too many things. The amount of toys and books in their rooms can be pretty overwhelming, so you will need to provide a good organization system.

Some families have playrooms full of toys. Often toys are all over the floor and create stress for parents. Once again, investing in some easy shelving and cabinet solutions will train your kids to be organized from an early age. It will be easier for you later and provide good life skills for them after they leave your home.

Children's Rooms Plants

Unless your child wants a plant, I would not put a live plant in their room. Their environments are already lively enough.

And now our journey takes us to a room that some people love very much and other people feel totally neutral about. And depending on the culture, for some, it is even considered to be a bad room. You can probably guess that we are entering the bathroom.

CHAPTER 16

Bathroom

I like to think about bathrooms, especially the master bathroom, as a sanctuary. They are not only functional rooms but can be created and treated as places of relaxation and rejuvenation for the body, mind, and spirit. In this age of busyness and chronic stress, it's essential that we take good care of our body and our mind. If the bathroom is pleasing and relaxing to your eyes and senses, it is more likely that you will want to spend a few extra minutes there to nourish yourself.

In a bathroom we are more tender and sensitive. We either like what we see in the mirror or we don't, so we can be emotional or even vulnerable. I invite you to create a room that resembles a spa.

> *If the environment is irresistibly beautiful and relaxing, you will be able to absorb the nourishing energy easily. As a result, even taking a shower or bath can become a ritual of giving yourself special care.*

Using a relaxing wall color, or a color that brings a sense of happiness, and adding plants and other natural elements will help to create the atmosphere of a sanctuary. If you are in an open and relaxed state of mind, water will work on you differently. The room will inspire you to slow down for a few minutes and do all the other good things you've been wanting to do for ages, like dry skin brushing, self-massage with warm oil, or a face mask.

Bathroom Colors

Designing bathrooms can be an inspiring project. Since it is your private area, you can experiment and implement colors and accents that really touch your heart and soul. It can be somewhat tricky to find a harmonious combination between the color of the walls, vanity, countertop, and floor tiles, but as long as it makes you happy, it doesn't have to be perfect. White or very dark vanities are easy as they go well with almost any color, and if your floor and vanity top is neutral enough, you have a lot of room to choose a fun color.

Although, as we discussed before, perception of color may vary from person to person. In general, light blue, aqua, warm gray, cream, tan, and soft green are relaxing colors and might work well for creating a spa atmosphere.

Soft green walls with yellow accents may contribute to a sense of vitality and playfulness if that is what you want.

If you often feel cold in a bathroom, choose a warmer, earthy color. I know some people don't like mauve colors, but it might be unexpected and interesting. And if you feel warm or even hot, a more cooling color like blue may work better for you.

You can use neutral tan or gray, but bring color with the wall tiles. Aqua glass tiles will look and feel wonderful with cool gray or warm tan colors.

Kid's restrooms benefit from being bright, well-lit, and cheerful. Yellows, bright Caribbean blues, and light greens will serve this purpose well.

Powder rooms are typically good rooms for using saturated colors. Do not be shy; engage your creativity, make a statement, and mostly have fun with it. A few rooms in the house are allowed to be unexpectedly colorful.

There are special cases when it is great to use rich and saturated colors in the bathroom to uplift the energy. This would be the case if your bathroom is located in the southeast (wealth), southwest (relationships), northwest (helpful people), or center of the house. Purple or green would be appropriate in the southeastern bathroom, green in the eastern bathroom, and yellow in the center, southwestern, and northwestern bathrooms.

Bathroom Furniture

Bathroom vanities have a huge price range and can be anywhere from simple and utilitarian to a piece of art. Spend some time looking around. While a white vanity fits with almost any bathroom interior, explore some natural wood options. A darker chestnut finish will stand out and look sharp and contemporary in any bathroom. Quartz or granite vanity tops can be incredibly beautiful and add a natural element to your sanctuary.

Bathroom Lighting

One important thing about bathroom lighting design is to avoid shadows. This is typically achieved by using a ceiling pendant or a chandelier and a light fixture above the mirror or two wall sconces on both sides of the mirror. There is an abundance of inexpensive and gorgeous bathroom light fixtures you can find online. If you feel like your bathroom light fixtures are old and you are tired of them, changing them all at once so you don't have to hire an electrician multiple times is a great way to bring some new energy into your bathroom. I recommend using soft white lights. Typically, you need brighter lighting for grooming, but it is too painful to use bright lights early in the morning or late at night, so a dimmer switch is a great idea in the bathroom.

Bathroom Art

Pictures of tropical flowers or trees, shells, and pebbles will look good and create the right atmosphere in a bathroom, reminding you of nature, the beach, and exotic vacations.

Bathroom Accessories

While white or cream towels and mats are easy and go well with everything, it might be fun to try different color floor mats and towels to create different moods. If your walls are green, you can use pink or lavender towels or mats. If your walls are blue, try cream or light yellow towels. Adding natural rocks or sea shells to your décor will bring nature and subconscious memories of a beach and vacation.

Bathroom Plants

My favorite plants in the bathroom are live orchids. If the space allows, and you have plenty of natural light, you can place any soft-looking green plants. Plants will thrive in humid environments. If there is not enough space, bring these natural vibes with pictures of plants.

If your bathroom is in the southeast, east, or south, use a picture or a mural of a tree, bamboo, or a flower with a long stem to lift the energy up. It's best if you place the picture above the toilet. If your bathroom is in the southwest or northwest, add some smooth river stones on both sides of your toilet or anywhere on the floor near the bathtub or sink to slow the energy down.

I hope implementing this idea of creating a sanctuary in your bathroom will help you to slow down and give yourself some well-deserved care. When I do follow-up sessions with my clients and they take me to their bathrooms, I can see their energy changes even upon entering the room. They instantly become more relaxed and happy and proud of their work. They usually smile.

We would not be able to move through the house were it not for the transitional places such as hallways and stairways, which is our next stop.

CHAPTER 17

Hallways, Stairways

Hallways and stairways are the channels in which energy moves throughout the house. The sense of harmony will be disturbed if the energy moves too fast or too slow, so it's best to get it right.

For example, in the narrow, long hallway, energy moves too fast and could even be "hitting" the room at the end of the hallway. Our intention will be to slow the energy down. This can be done with art, mirrors, runners, and lighting. If you place a painting on one wall and a mirror on the opposite wall, the space will feel larger, which will help to slow down the energy. The wavy or perpendicular-to-the-flow pattern of a runner helps to slow the energy down even more. If there is a chandelier or pendant in the way of the flow, it also creates a further slow-down effect.

Another common scenario of the energy moving too fast is when you see the back sliding door or a large window from the main entryway. In traditional feng shui this represents money rushing out of the house too fast. I am not sure if it relates to money specifically. Usually if there are financial troubles, there are several reasons for it, and it is hard to separate their influence. But what's happening in the case of seeing the back glass door or window from the entrance is that the energy doesn't have a chance to accumulate in the house to nourish the structure and its residents.

Often other rooms feel energetically lower or more yin than they should where the energy moves too quickly. You can work on increasing the energy in other rooms, but you can also attempt to slow the energy down at the entrance. You can place a round table in the entryway between the front door and the large back window or sliding door. You can keep a large bouquet of flowers, a few orchids, or other favorite plants on the table. Placing a rug and hanging a chandelier may also help to slow the energy down. Another solution is to place a tall, lush plant in front of the back window. Choose the way that is most aesthetically appropriate for you and your home.

There are a number of houses to which this rule doesn't apply, such as houses located on oceans or lakes. Often these homes have incredible views. To see the view upon entering the house, architects put a large window right across from the front door. I've observed some of these houses for a while, and I don't see that this principle works the same way here. In cases like these, expansive water views energize the house. The whole property has a very strong energy, at times much stronger than any normal location. In addition, every room with windows facing the ocean receives a significant amount of energy as well. Similarly, houses with incredible views of meadows or hills with distant mountain ranges are nourished by the strong energy of the mountains. In fact, mountains provide strengthening and hold energy at the back of the house, so I would not be concerned with seeing such a view upon entering the house. I am not saying that it is the best architectural approach. There are other ways to experience incredible views; they don't have to be seen right after you open the front door.

Every house and its surrounding land are unique, and the overall energy consists of many different ingredients. The individual approach provides the best results.

Hallway and Stairway Colors

Transitional areas are connected to other rooms and spaces. It is best if the wall color of these areas is light and neutral. It should be a color that doesn't clash and is in harmony with the colors of other rooms that are visible from these transitional areas. Most often, I use neutral off-white colors in these areas. The color must work well with all the rest of the colors and can be used in the main entrance, stairway, second-floor landing, and all the hallways.

Hallways, Stairway Furniture, and Lighting

It's rare that we place any furniture in the hallway unless it is wide enough to have a bookshelf or a thin console table, but art, mirrors, or runners are appropriate here.

We discussed stairway lighting in the Entryway chapter. As for hallways, it is best to have them moderately but not excessively lit either with recessed lighting or wall sconces. If your hallway is an art gallery or a place where you hang family photos, consider implementing track lighting or angled recessed lights.

Hallways, Stairway Art, and Accessories

If it is a darker hallway, use lighter and brighter-colored art. Since most hallways can fit more than one picture, display a theme there such as nature, flowers, boats, etc. Create a family gallery or your adventures wall on the second floor landing wall. They don't have to be the same size; you can artistically arrange them in a random pattern. This can be your private family gallery, and you can keep adding pictures of your kids or your new adventures.

Do not place pictures in an ascending pattern following the stairway. It makes the stairway look steeper.

If there is a wall at the end of a long hallway, place a bright picture there. It will help to make the hallway feel shorter. You can also place a small table with a table lamp or a statue there.

Stairways and landings don't require accessories, but if there is plenty of space, use your creativity and imagination and place a special item there that brings you joy.

Hallways and Stairway Plants

If your entryway is open to the second floor, place a plant on the second-floor landing. It will look great from the first floor and welcome you to the second floor. The ZZ plant doesn't require too much light or too much space and has nice rounded leaves, which makes it a perfect choice for a stairway landing.

I hope understanding the functionality of the transitional spaces will help you to manage the energy in your home better, therefore creating more balance and bringing more harmony.

The last stop in our journey is the home office. I put it at the end because not everyone has a separate room for a home office, yet with the increased working-from-home lifestyle, it is important to have a designated area in the home where we work.

CHAPTER 18

Home Office or Space Designated for Work

The importance of a well-functioning home office or working-from-home designated area became apparent during the COVID-19 pandemic. While consulting for my clients, I see many different scenarios of how people work from home. Many do not have a regular desk and migrate throughout the day with their laptop from the dining table to the couch and even the bed. Others use their dining room table more permanently. Some people squeeze a small desk in their guest bedroom while others land in the basement. Surprisingly, all of this happened not only in small homes and apartments but in large homes too. Although some of these scenarios are better than others, none of them are ideal.

If you want to be productive, creative, and minimize your levels of stress, you must have an environment that supports you. You need to give it some thought and invest time to create a better workspace for yourself. I am absolutely certain it will pay off in a big way. After all, this is the space where you make money! Here are a few things to consider.

Having a designated separate room is definitely a big plus and should be your goal. After all, your work is the most important activity after sleeping and eating. Yes, it is convenient to be able to close the door when you need to make client conference calls, but there is so much more to it. When we use a room for a particular activity, the energy is cultivated by repeating that activity. It doesn't feel right to work in a bedroom or kitchen, right? Because the energy there is set up for a different activity. The same principle applies to the office. Work is very different from resting, eating, or sleeping.

> *It is best to keep work separate from your living space, otherwise seeing your desk or work-related items from your living space will always remind you about unfinished projects and more work that can be done, which means that it will be harder to relax and recharge your batteries.*

Some basements with large windows or sliding doors would be appropriate for an office because they have plenty of vital energy and often beautiful garden views, but many basements have small windows or no windows, their energy is low and often heavy, so most likely, you will feel drained after spending several hours working there. Besides, air is often more humid and stale in basements. Some finished attic spaces might work, too, but they usually get too hot in the summer or too cold in the winter. In addition, they have slanted ceilings and beams. If the temperature is not a problem and this area might work for you, see the discussion on desk placement below.

Some homes have game rooms above the garage. Usually game rooms are not used too often and there's good potential for creating an office there. I highly recommend separating an area of the room with a divider for your work-designated space rather than just placing a desk in the corner of a large room.

Depending on your family circumstances, part of your living room, dining room, or other appropriate room that is not used too often can be used as a work area too. It is best to avoid working in the bedroom where you sleep. If you have a large one-bedroom or studio apartment, and the bedroom is the only place where you can set up your office, you must place a screen between your bed and desk. Please review Chapter 14 on bedrooms. However, if you have a guest bedroom and guests only stay once or twice a year for holidays, it could be a promising space to set up your work area. We will discuss desk placement in the Furniture section later in this chapter.

Home Office Colors

If you work from home full-time, it could mean that you spend six to ten hours in this room daily. A home office color must be supportive of your energy and pleasing to your senses. Here are a few helpful but general guidelines:

- ▶ If the room is too small, choose a lighter and brighter color.
- ▶ If the room is in the northern part of the house, choose a warmer and lighter color.
- ▶ If the room is in the southern part of the house and very bright, using a darker and less saturated color would be more balancing.
- ▶ Blues would be too cold and too relaxing for the home office. However, most people like blues, so if you end up with a choice of blue, make sure it is a warmer and softer shade of blue.
- ▶ Grays and beiges are uninspiring and boring. You need more stimulation in the office than these colors can provide. If you still want to use them, make sure to use art with bright colors on the walls and live plants.
- ▶ Light and warm greens or sage greens, depending on the shade, can be soothing, balancing, or energizing to your system and can be a good choice.
- ▶ Reds are overly stimulating and too aggressive for the office. However, the right amount of stimulation is a plus, as it inspires creativity and uplifts the mood. If you feel an affinity with lilac, purple, pink, or orange colors, choose the shade that is not very saturated and on the softer side. Sometimes a bright, strongly colored accent wall works well, especially for people who are doing creative work.

Home Office Furniture

Desk Placement

The majority of people sit in their home office facing a wall like it is drawn in position 3 of the diagram. If we sit in our office facing a wall, we feel restricted and less creative. If this is the only way your space allows you to place your desk, place a picture with an open view in front of you.

Some people sit in front of the window with their back exposed to the door or with their back to the window. See position 1-2 in the diagram. In both of these positions we feel vulnerable, because our back is unprotected.

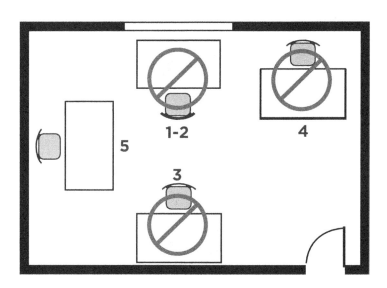

Diagram 15: Home office desk placement

If you must sit with your back to the window, try to move your desk away from the window and consider placing a console cabinet between your chair and the window. It would also help to have an office chair with a tall, solid back.

Sitting with your back to the door is the worst position, but if you must, place a small mirror that reflects the door. This way you can detect movement and see who is entering.

Sometimes people sit right in front of the door like in position 4. This is not ideal because the energy rushes straight onto you. This could result in getting tired or agitated more easily.

In order to have a good flow of creative, supportive energy and feel strong and productive, it is best to have an open space in front of us and a solid wall behind us. It is best to sit diagonally from the door and have a window to our side. This way we feel secure, relaxed, and empowered. We can see who is entering and can enjoy nature through the window. Position 5 in the diagram is called the power position.

If you work from the living room or dining room, you can try and choose the corner that allows you to sit in this position rather than with your back to the door.

If your work area is in the guest bedroom, typically the size of the room will not allow you to have both the bed and the desk placed in the power position. In this case, you have to prioritize the desk placement. You may need to sacrifice the bed and instead get a sleeper sofa for your guests. A sofa would be a good piece of furniture in your office and a comfortable place for your guests to sleep. With some creative thinking and a little bit of money spent, you will have a supportive place to work from. All you need is to prioritize it.

If you have a slanted ceiling, it's pretty bad if you sit facing the wall and the slanted ceiling is right in front of you, almost pressing on your head. You must place your desk closer to the center of the room, or far enough from the wall to be able to put a chair and not hit your head when you stand up. It's not so bad if the lowest part is behind you.

If there is a beam in your ceiling, try to place the desk so the beam does not cross your desk, or at least your head.

To the best of your ability, try to place your desk away from any sharp, triangular architectural and design details. At least make sure that the sharp features and corners are not pointed at your head. Open shelves would be in that category as well. Avoid sharp vertical shades in the windows or sliding doors. Use softer shades instead.

Desk Material, Color, and Size

Natural wood by far is your best choice. Much research has shown that seeing a wood grain de-stresses us. According to environmental psychologist Sally Augustine, "seeing real and artificial wood grain has the same effect on us as long as two things are true: the artificial wood is a really, truly good imitation of natural wood and the repeat pattern in the artificial wood is random enough." Lighter or medium-colored desks such as maple, cherry, or walnut where you can see the grain and patterns in the wood are best.

Glass is not a good material for the desk or any other kind of table. It is hard and cold, and it doesn't hold energy. Metal is also hard and cold and not appropriate for the desk.

The size of the desk should be proportional to your size and the size of the room. If the desk is too big or too small for the room it will feel out of place, and every time you enter the room, you will feel that something is off. You do not want to start your workday with this feeling. I see desks that are too small way more often than desks that are too large. If your desk is too small, you will not be able to spread your energy, and you will be reminded all the time that you are restricted and limited. This will likely influence your performance and feeling of self-worth.

Ergonomics

Your desk and computer chair should be the right height for you. The chair should have lumbar support and armrests. It is worth it to spend the time and try different settings on your chair and armrest height and observe how it feels on your back, shoulders, and neck. Sometimes putting a small pillow behind your back can make a difference whether you have back pain or not. Sometimes it is worth getting a special lumbar pillow.

Home Office Lighting

We already discussed the importance of positioning your desk by the window to maximize your exposure to natural light. When the day is overcast, you may need an additional source of ambient lighting. For a larger space, it can be recessed lighting; for smaller rooms, a ceiling pendant will be fine. You need to make sure the light source is not reflected in your monitor.

For task lighting, I prefer two LED lamps on both sides of my desk. I use a desk lamp closer to my monitor and a floor lamp on the other side of my desk. This way my work area is illuminated on both sides, which helps to minimize shadows. Both lamps have different settings of colder or warmer types of lighting and a dimmer.

Art and Accessories

As with color, a lot goes into choosing a piece of art or a photograph that is right for you and your office. One of the aspects of it is a certain personal connection to the place depicted in a photo or painting, or a piece that contains a positive emotion of some kind. It could be an amazing nature scene from a place you love. It could be something you want. For example, if you want a vacation home on a lake, or you associate money with freedom to travel to certain places, put a picture reminding you of it in your office. Some people like cars or boats, some get inspired by nature. It is good to ask yourself what you want. Why do you work hard besides being able to pay bills and provide necessities for yourself and your family? What is your inspiration in life? This special piece of art could depict that. If you place it on the wall in front of you, or anywhere you can see it from your desk, it will remind you of the reward for your hard work.

Plants

I cannot emphasize enough the importance and positivity of plants. There is plenty of research that shows a connection with increased productivity and well-being in the office when plants are introduced. This applies to the home office as well. In addition to absorbing carbon dioxide and producing oxygen, plants absorb electromagnetic radiation from all our devices. They also clean the air of toxic substances that come from furniture off-gassing and household cleaners. I usually suggest placing one or two plants close to the area where your computer, printer, and other electronic devices are stationed.

A Special Word on Clutter in the Office

It is a great practice to declutter and tidy up your office occasionally. Often home offices are full of papers and things, and this stagnates the energy. There is no one good rule for everyone on how often to declutter, but I guarantee, every time you declutter, you will feel more energy and a burst of good mood and creativity to support you in your work. Personally, I feel irritated and uninspired when my space is cluttered. Some creative clutter is okay during a special project, as long as it gets sorted out before too long. And don't forget the closet! Imagine how much of your energy will free up when you let go of things and papers you don't need anymore.

It is enjoyable and rewarding to have a clean, functional, and uplifting workspace. If the weather permits, open the windows to get fresh air and hear the sounds of nature. Occasionally, place flowers or a small plant on your desk.

I cannot even count how many times I have heard from my clients that making changes in their home office or creating a designated work area helped them to be more productive, creative, and relaxed, and as a result, get raises, promotions, more visibility, and respect within the company. What stands out to me is they felt more confident and happier overall.

Final Thoughts

If you transform your home into a soulful space that vibrates with frequencies of joy, contentment, and love that is always inside you underneath the fear, tension, stress, and dissatisfaction, your life will change, and this change will be permanent. Your home will continuously reflect who you really are.

Everything is connected. If enough people transform their homes into soulful spaces, this goodness, kindness, and love will spread and the Earth, our bigger home, will become a better place for everyone. Let it begin in your home, in one room. Bring love to one room, and it will spread. Love is an open concept. It cannot be contained; it needs to be expressed and shared.

Your life can be beautiful, and your new story can be as magical and fulfilling as you allow it to be. Transformation is only possible if you really want it and put your will into staying on the task.

Be spontaneous, playful, and real. Do not be afraid to make mistakes. Allow yourself to be *you*. It is my hope that you will discover more of who you are in this process of creating a soulful home.

With great love,
Natalia

About the Author

NATALIA KAYLIN has over two decades of experience as an educator and practitioner in creating beautiful, well-functioning, and supportive environments. She applies her knowledge of feng shui, environmental psychology, and design sensibility to help clients obtain transformative and sustainable results for their homes.

Natalia has an MS in physics and came to the field of conscious design from an electro-optical engineering background. She has also studied with renowned feng shui masters and holds several certifications, including the Certificate of Advanced Feng Shui Studies in China.

Natalia has taught workshops at the University of Massachusetts, Williams College, and the Build Boston convention. Her articles have appeared in numerous publications, and she has been interviewed about feng shui and conscious design by several media outlets.

Natalia combines her passion for beautiful spaces, her expertise in Eastern esotericism, and a love of science to achieve unique and empowering designs. She has helped thousands of people discover their strength, creativity, and joy by changing their homes.

Natalia founded her practice, Natalia Kaylin Feng Shui Consulting and Design, in 2002. She lives in Massachusetts and is on a quest to share her passion for creating soulful homes with people all around the globe.

Visit Natalia online at www.nataliakaylin.com.

Made in the USA
Coppell, TX
30 December 2022

10091782R00138